AMERICAN STANDARD MEASUREMENTS

Apart from tabelspoons and teaspoons, which are roughly equivalent to metric/ imperial tablespoons and teaspoons, wherever possible, Americans measure in cups. A standard American measuring cup holds 8 fl oz (about 225 ml). Although the weights of foods will vary considerably, they fall into roughly two categories, those that weigh about 8 ounces (225 g) and those that weigh about 4 ounces (115 g).

Foods that weigh approximately 8 ounces (225 g) per cup are sugar, butter, rice and other whole grains and beans.

Foods that weigh approximately 4 ounces (115 g) are flours of all grades, mushrooms and ground almonds.

The USDA supplies standard cup measurement equivalent for most foods, but the conversion from a weighed amount can never be 100% accurate.

It is very important to notice that American standard liquid measurements are not the same as Imperial liquid measurements, because an American pint is only 16 fluid ounces, instead of 20 fluid ounces, the Imperial pint. Thus an American pint is equal to two American cups.

DR. OETKER

GERMAN BAKING TODAY

THE ORIGINAL

DR. OETKER

GERMAN BAKING TODAY

THE ORIGINAL

CERES

Foreword

'The Pleasures of Baking' has long been a standard work for German home bakers and those who enjoy baking Continental cakes, biscuits and pastries.

In this revised edition, some old recipes that had almost been forgotten have been revived and new recipes from all over Germany have been added.

Thanks to the step-by-step photos and our detailed instructions, even inexperienced bakers can be confident of success. Some of the latest ideas, tried and tested in Dr. Oetker's test kitchen, have been included in the revised recipes.

Whether you want to try your hand at a classic marble cake, fruit tartlets or a poppyseed strudel, you will certainly be inspired by this wide-ranging selection of recipes.

We wish you 'good appetite' in sampling the delicious results of your labours.

CONTENTS

QUARK AND OIL DOUGH

CHOUX PASTE

STRUDEL DOUGH

COMBINED DOUGHS

PUFF PASTE

MERINGUE

DEEP-FRIED PASTRIES

CHRISTMAS BAKING

BREAD DOUGHS

Pages 280 – 293

Before you start baking

Mixing flour and baking powder.
If cornflour or cocoa powder are included in the ingredients, they should be mixed in with the flour (except in the case of Marble Cake).

Sifting flour and baking powder.
The sifting process separates the grains of flour and distributes the baking powder evenly throughout the flour. This gives a good even texture to the cake.
When using baking powder and wholemeal flour, just mix them together, do not sift them. Since wholemeal flour has a much coarser consistency, it tends to lump together.

When baking a cake batter, use a pastry brush to grease the tin generously and evenly with soft margarine or butter. Do not use oil as it will run down the sides of the tin.
If you wish, you can sprinkle biscuit or cake crumbs over the inside surfaces.
If using a loose-bottomed or springform tin, grease the base only, not the sides.

If you are baking in a loaf-tin, you can line it with non-stick baking paper. The cake can then be removed from the tin more easily and it will also stay fresh longer.
To make the paper lining, place the base of the loaf-tin on the paper and draw round it. Tip the tin on its side and mark out the side dimensions. Repeat the process with the other three sides. Cut out the corners and fold along the base lines.

The method

Getting the margarine or butter to the right consistency.
It is most important to ensure that the fat is not too soft or too firm. A fat which is runny will never produce a smooth batter. A hard fat must be softened in advance. To do this, warm the mixing bowl in hot water and then work the fat thoroughly by hand. Once it can be easily moulded, cream the fat in a food processor or using the whisk attachment on a hand-blender at high speed.

Gradually add the sugar and vanilla sugar to the creamed fat.
Add the sugars a tablespoon at a time and stir carefully. The vanilla sugar, can be replaced by vanilla essence but this must be added when you add the eggs or other liquid.

When using honey, this too must be stirred in gradually. Cakes containing honey have a tendency to become dry and also to burn, make sure you do not bake them any longer than the recipe specifies.

Adding spices and flavourings.
Beat the mixture until light and fluffy. Caster sugar is preferable to granulated sugar as it dissolves more easily.
When using honey, thick honey is preferable to clear honey.

Adding eggs.
Always break each egg into a cup first to check that it is usable. Never add the eggs all at once into the creamed fat and sugar (or honey), or they will not blend in well. Always beat in each egg for about 30 seconds before adding the next. The fat and sugar/honey mixture should be light and fluffy. If the eggs are too cold, the mixture may curdle and this will spoil the appearance of the finished product, so do not use eggs straight from the refrigerator.

Stirring in the flour and baking powder.
Stir the flour, which has been mixed and sifted with the baking powder, into the creamed fat and beat at medium speed. If the mixture is too firm, add a little water. Baking powder should never come into direct contact with liquid, or its raising properties will be lost too soon. If extra flour (or milk) has to be added to the mixture, stir only for a short time, or air bubbles may cause the cake to develop an irregular texture. Blend the finished mixture at medium speed.

Only use as much milk as is necessary to give the mixture a slow dropping consistency.
The quantity of milk required depends on the absorbency of the flour as well as the size of the eggs. The mixture has just the right consistency when it drops from a spoon with a firm or slow dropping consistency. If too much milk is added, then the baked cake may contain streaks of water. The only cake batter that can be softer in texture is one which uses a lot of fat and eggs and little or no liquid. This is because the eggs will firm up from the heat generated during the baking process.

Stir fruit into the mixture as directed in the recipe.
Stir the fruit into the cake mixture at medium speed. If the mixture is beaten for too long, the fruit will break up and lend an unattractive colour to the mixture.

Transferring the batter to the prepared tin.
Fill the greased tin with the batter (preferably using a dough scraper or plastic spatula) and level off the surface. Tins should only be filled about two-thirds full.

Baking cake batters

Cake batters must go into the oven as soon as they are ready. Always follow the directions given in the recipe.
Turn out cakes baked in moulded tins, such as gugelhupf tins or ring moulds, 10 minutes after they come out of the oven and place on a cooling rack. Cakes baked in plain cake tins should be turned out immediately.

Basic recipe
Grundrezept

250 g (9 oz) margarine or butter
200 g (7 oz) sugar
2 tsp vanilla sugar
1 pinch salt
5 eggs
500 g (1 lb 2 oz) plain flour
15 g (1 tbsp) baking powder
about 50 ml (2 fl oz) milk

Use a food processor or the whisk attachment on a hand-mixer at high speed to cream the margarine or butter and then gradually add the sugar, vanilla sugar and a pinch of salt. Continue to beat until the mixture is light and fluffy. Add the eggs as you beat (one every 30 seconds or so). Mix the flour and baking powder and sift them. Gradually add the dry ingredients and milk to the creamed fat beating continuously at medium speed. Only use as much milk as is necessary to give the mixture a slow dropping consistency.
Transfer the mixture to a prepared cake tin (such as a gugelhupf tin 22-24 cm (9 inch) in diameter), place in the oven and bake for the time and at the temperature specified in the recipe

or

for smaller quantities

125 g ($4\frac{1}{2}$ oz) margarine or butter
100 g ($3\frac{1}{2}$) oz sugar
2 tsp vanilla sugar
1 pinch salt
3 eggs
250 g (9 oz) plain flour
3 tsp baking powder
about 2 tbsp milk

Use a food processor or the whisk attachment on a hand-mixer at high speed to cream the margarine or butter and then gradually add the sugar, vanilla sugar and a pinch of salt. Continue to beat until the mixture is light and fluffy. Add the eggs as you beat (one every 30 seconds or so). Sift together the flour and baking powder. Add this and the milk to the creamed fat a little at a time, beating continuously at medium speed. Only use as much milk as is necessary to give the mixture a slow dropping consistency.
Transfer the mixture into a prepared 30 cm (12 inch) diameter sponge tin with 11 cm (4 inch) sides or a Swiss roll tin.

Marble Cake

Marmorkuchen (Cover Photo)

traditional

300 g (10½ oz) margarine or butter
275 g (9½ oz) sugar
2 tsp vanilla sugar
½ tsp rum essence
1 pinch salt
5 eggs
375 g (13 oz) plain flour
4 tsp baking powder
about 3 tbsp milk

Use the whisk on a hand mixer or a food processor to cream the margarine or butter, then gradually add the sugar, vanilla sugar, rum essence and a pinch of salt. Continue to beat until the mixture is light and fluffy. Add the eggs as you beat (one every 30 seconds or so). Mix and sift the flour and baking powder. Gradually add the milk to the creamed fat, beating continuously at medium speed. Only use as much milk as is necessary to give the mixture a slow dropping consistency.

Transfer two-thirds of the mixture into a greased 22-24 cm (8-9 inch) cake tin.

4 tsp cocoa powder
4 tsp sugar
2–3 tbsp milk

Sift together the cocoa powder and sugar and add to the remaining third of the mixture, together with the milk. Beat until the mixture returns to a slow dropping consistency. Spread the chocolate-coloured mixture over the light mixture and then lightly swirl the two together with a fork to create a marbling effect.

Oven temperatures

Conventional oven about 180°C/350°F (preheated)
Fan-assisted oven about 160°C/325°F (not preheated)
Gas oven mark 2–3 (not preheated)
Baking time 50-65 minutes.

30 g (1 oz) icing sugar

Dust the cooled cake with icing sugar.

Variation

4 tbsp apricot jam (warmed and sieved)
1 tbsp water

Bake the mixture in a 35 cm (14 inch) long greased Swiss roll tin with 11 cm (4 inch) high sides. When cool, coat with apricot glaze.
To make the apricot glaze put the warmed, sieved apricot jam in a saucepan, add the water, boil and reduce slightly. Brush the surface of the cake with the glaze.

Saddle of Venison Cake

popular

Rehrücken (see photo on pages 10/11)

For the mixture

100 g (3½ oz) margarine or butter	Use the whisk attachment on a hand mixer at high speed to cream the margarine or butter and then gradually add the sugar, vanilla sugar and a pinch of salt. Continue to beat until the mixture is light and fluffy. Add the eggs as you beat (one every 30 seconds or so). Stir in the grated chocolate. Sift together the flour, baking powder and chocolate pudding powder; then add the dry ingredients and milk to the creamed fat a little at a time, beating continuously on medium speed. Only use as much milk as is necessary to give the mixture a slow dropping consistency.
150 g (5½ oz) sugar	
2 tsp vanilla sugar	
1 pinch salt	
3 eggs	
100 g (3½ oz) grated chocolate	
50 g (2 oz) plain flour	
1 packet chocolate pudding powder	
2 tsp baking powder	Stir in the blanched, ground almonds and then transfer the mixture into a greased 'saddle of venison' cake tin (a ridged mould) measuring 30 x 11 cm (12 x 28 inch). Level off the surface.
2 tbsp milk	
75 g (2¾ oz) blanched ground almonds	

Oven temperatures	
Conventional oven	170–200°C/350–400°F (preheated)
Fan-assisted oven	150–160°C/300–325°F (not preheated)
Gas oven	mark 2-3 (not preheated)
Baking time	50–60 minutes.

Leave the cake to stand for 10 minutes, turn it out of the tin and leave to cool.

For the icing

100 g (3½ oz) plain cooking chocolate	Break up the chocolate and melt it, together with the creamed coconut, over a low heat in a bain-marie. Stir the chocolate mixture until it thickens. When the cake has cooled, coat it with the icing and then stud with the slivered almonds.
4 tsp creamed coconut	
40 g (1½ oz) slivered almonds	

Variation

4–5 tbsp apricot jam	For an even tastier Saddle of Venison cake, coat the cake with apricot syrup as soon as it comes out of the oven.
1 tbsp water	To make the syrup, press the apricot jam through a sieve, add the water, bring to the boil and reduce the liquid slightly. Spread the syrup over the surface of the cake when still hot. Leave to cool before icing the cake.

Rich Nut Cake

Saftiger Nußkuchen

popular

For the mixture

125 g (4½ oz) margarine or butter 125 g (4½ oz) sugar 2 tsp vanilla sugar 1 tbsp rum essence 1 pinch salt 8 egg yolks 300 g (10½ oz) ground hazelnuts 50 g (2 oz) chopped hazelnuts 1 tsp baking powder 8 egg whites	Use the whisk attachment on a hand mixer at high speed or a food processor to cream the margarine or butter, then gradually add the sugar, vanilla sugar, rum essence and a pinch of salt. Continue to beat until the mixture is light and fluffy. Add the egg yolks as you beat (one every 30 seconds or so). Combine the ground and chopped hazelnuts and the baking powder and then beat them at medium speed in three separate portions into the creamed fat. Whisk the egg whites until stiff and fold them into the mixture. Line the base and sides of a 26 cm (10 inch) springform tin with non-stick baking paper. Grease the paper on the base. Transfer the mixture to the tin.
Oven temperatures	
Conventional oven	about 170°C/350°F (preheated)
Fan-assisted oven	about 150°C/325°F (not preheated)
Gas oven	mark 2-3 (not preheated)
Baking time	45-55 minutes. Release the spring on the tin, remove the cake and leave to cool on a wire rack.

For the icing

250 g (9 oz) icing sugar 1 tbsp rum water 75 g (2¾ oz) coarsely-chopped hazelnuts	Sift the icing sugar and add the rum and water, stirring until the mixture is smooth and thick. Spread it over the surface of the cake and then sprinkle with the coarsely chopped hazelnuts.
Tip	Instead of icing the Rich Nut Cake, you could coat it with whole-milk chocolate cake covering (about 300 g (10½ oz)).

Delicious Apple Cake

easy

Apfelkuchen, sehr fein

For the mixture

125 g (4½ oz) margarine or butter
125 g (4½ oz) sugar
2 tsp vanilla sugar
¼ tsp lemon essence
1 pinch salt
3 eggs
200 g (7 oz) plain flour
2 tsp baking powder
1–2 tbsp milk

Use an electric whisk or food processor to cream the margarine or butter at high speed, then gradually add the sugar, vanilla sugar, the lemon essence and a pinch of salt. Continue to beat until the mixture is light and fluffy. Add the eggs as you beat (one every 30 seconds or so). In a bowl, sift together the flour and the baking powder. Gradually add them and the milk to the creamed fat, beating continuously at medium speed. Only use as much milk as is necessary to give the mixture a slow dropping consistency.

Transfer the mixture into a 28 cm (11 inch) springform tin and level off the surface with a spatula.

For the topping

750 g (1 lb 10 oz) apples
25 g (1 oz) melted butter
40 g (1½ oz) sultanas (optional)

Peel, quarter and core the apples. Make a few parallel cuts on the peeled sides of the apple quarters and then arrange them in a flower-shape on top of the mixture. Melt the butter and brush the apples with it. Sprinkle with the sultanas, if using.

Oven temperatures	
Conventional oven	about 180°C/350°F (preheated)
Fan-assisted oven	about 160°C/325°C (not preheated)
Gas oven	mark 2–3 (not preheated)
Baking time	40-50 minutes.

For the apricot syrup

2 tbsp apricot jam (strained through a sieve)
1 tbsp water

To make the syrup, press the apricot jam through a sieve, add a little water, boil and reduce slightly. Spread the syrup on to the surface of the cake as soon as it comes out of the oven.

Variation Instead of apples, use 600 g (1lb 5 oz) morello cherries.

Fried Egg Cake

Spiegeleierkuchen

easy

For the topping

2 packets vanilla pudding powder
80 g (3 oz) sugar
750 ml (1¼ pints) milk

Follow the instructions for making the vanilla puddings but use only 750 ml (1¼ pints) milk. Leave to cool, stirring from time to time.

For the batter

150 g (5½ oz) margarine or butter
150 g (5½ oz) sugar
2 tsp vanilla sugar
1 pinch salt
3 eggs
300 g (10½ oz) plain flour
2 tsp baking powder
2 tbsp milk
500 ml (18 fl oz) crème fraîche
700 g (1lb 9 oz) canned apricots

Use the whisk attachment on a hand blender at high speed to cream the margarine or butter and then gradually add the sugar, vanilla sugar and a pinch of salt. Continue to beat until the mixture is light and fluffy. Add the eggs as you beat (one every 30 seconds or so).
Sift together the flour and the baking powder. Add this and the milk to the creamed fat a little at a time, beating continuously at medium speed.
Spread on to a greased baking sheet. Fold a strip of aluminium foil several times and then arrange it around the mixture to hold it in place.
Stir the crème fraîche into the cooled pudding and spread this evenly over the mixture (photo 1).
Drain the canned apricots, reserving 500 ml (18 fl oz) of the juice. Arrange the apricots cut side down on the white pudding (photo 2).

Oven temperatures

Conventional oven	170–200°C/350–400°F (preheated)
Fan-assisted oven	150–170°C/300–325°F (not preheated)
Gas oven	mark 3–4 (preheated)
Baking time	about 30 minutes.

Leave to cool.

For the glaze

2 packets quick jelly glaze
50 g (2 oz) sugar
500 ml (18 fl oz) apricot juice

Make the glaze as directed on the packet instructions, using the sugar and the reserved juice from the canned apricots. Spread it over the topping (photo 3) and leave to set.

Ottilie Cake
Ottilienkuchen

250 g (9 oz) margarine or butter **200 g (7 oz) sugar** **2 tsp vanilla sugar** **¼ tsp rum essence** **1 pinch salt**	Use the whisk attachment on a hand blender at high speed or a food processor to cream the margarine or butter and then gradually add the sugar, vanilla sugar, the rum flavouring and a pinch of salt.
4 eggs **200 g (7 oz) plain flour** **50 g (2 oz) cornflour** **1 tsp baking powder** **100 g (3½ oz) cooking chocolate**	Continue to beat until the mixture is light and fluffy. Add the eggs as you beat (one every 30 seconds or so). Sift together the flour, cornflour and the baking powder. Add this to the creamed fat, beating at medium speed.
100 g (3½ oz) blanched ground almonds **50 g (2 oz) finely chopped crystallised citron or lemon peel**	Break up the chocolate and add to the mixture, together with the blanched, ground almonds and chopped crystallised citron or lemon peel, beating carefully at medium speed. Transfer the mixture into a greased 30 x 11 cm (12 x 4 inch) cake tin, lined with non-stick baking paper.
Oven temperatures	
Conventional oven	160–180°C/325–350°F (preheated)
Fan-assisted oven	150–160°C/300–325°F (not preheated)
Gas oven	mark 2–3 (not preheated)
Baking time	65–75 minutes.
Icing sugar	Remove the cake from the tin, leave to cool and dust with icing sugar.

King cake
Königskuchen

300 g (10½ oz) margarine or butter **250 g (9 oz) sugar** **2 tsp vanilla sugar** **¼ tsp lemon essence or** **½ tsp rum essence** **1 pinch salt** **5 eggs** **500 g (1 lb 2 oz) plain flour** **4 tsp baking powder** **2–3 tbsp milk** **250 g (9 oz) raisins** **50 g (2 oz) finely chopped crystallised citron or lemon peel**	Use the whisk attachment on a hand blender at high speed to cream the margarine or butter then gradually add the sugar, vanilla sugar, the lemon or rum essence and a pinch of salt. Continue to beat until the mixture is light and fluffy. Add the eggs as you beat (one every 30 seconds or so). Sift together the flour and the baking powder. Add this and the milk to the creamed fat a little at a time, beating continuously at medium speed. Only use as much milk as is necessary to give the mixture a slow dropping consistency.

(continued on page 26)

50 g (2 oz) glacé cherries, coarsely chopped	Carefully beat the raisins, crystallised lemon and glacé cherries into the mixture at medium speed. Transfer to a 35 x 11 cm (14 x 4 inch) greased cake tin, lined with non-stick baking paper.

Oven temperatures

Conventional oven	160–180°C/325–350°F (preheated)
Fan-assisted oven	140–150°C/300–325°F (not preheated)
Gas oven	mark 2–3 (not preheated)
Baking time	about 80 minutes.

Crumble Cake with Apple Filling

easy

Krümelkuchen mit Apfelfüllung

For the crumb mixture

- 250 g (9 oz) margarine or butter
- 200 g (7 oz) sugar
- 2 tsp vanilla sugar
- 1 pinch salt
- 1 egg
- 500 g (1 lb 2 oz) plain flour
- 15 g(1 tbsp) baking powder

Use the whisk attachment on a hand blender at high speed to cream the margarine or butter and then gradually add the sugar, vanilla sugar and a pinch of salt. Continue to beat until the mixture is light and fluffy. Add the egg as you beat (for about 30 seconds). Sift together the flour and the baking powder. Beat half of the flour into the creamed fat at medium speed. Add the rest of the flour, using the hand mixer with a kneading hook, until the mixture resembles coarse breadcrumbs.

For the filling

- 1 1/2–2 kg (3 1/2-4 lb) cooking apples
- 1 tbsp water
- about 150 g (5 1/2 oz) sugar
- 30 g (1 oz) butter
- 1 pinch ground cinnamon
- 75 g (2 3/4 oz) raisins

Peel, quarter, core and chop the apples. Add the water, sugar, butter, ground cinnamon and raisins . Cook over a low heat until soft, stirring gently. Leave to cool, adding a little sugar to taste, if necessary.

Assembling the cake

Place half the crumb mixture on a greased baking sheet. Press down firmly and raise the edges by about 5 mm (¼ inch). Fold a piece of aluminium foil several times and place around the mixture. Spread the apple mixture evenly over the crumble and then sprinkle the rest of the crumble on top.

Oven temperatures

Conventional oven	170–200°C/350–400°F (preheated)
Fan-assisted oven	160–170°C/325°F (not preheated)
Gas oven	mark 3-4 (not preheated)
Baking time	35–45 minutes.

Rondo Cake
Rodonkuchen

For the mixture

- 250 g (9 oz) margarine or butter
- 200 g (7 oz) sugar
- 2 tsp vanilla sugar
- 1 pinch salt
- 5 eggs
- 500 g (1lb 2 oz) plain flour
- 15 g (1 tbsp) baking powder
- about 50 ml (2 fl oz) milk
- 150 g (5½ oz) currants
- 150 g (5½ oz) raisins

Use the whisk attachment on a hand mixer at high speed or a food processor to cream the margarine or butter. Gradually add the sugar, vanilla sugar and a pinch of salt. Continue to beat until the mixture is light and fluffy. Add the eggs as you beat (one every 30 seconds or so). Sift the flour and baking powder together. Add this and then the milk to the creamed fat, a little at a time, beating continuously at medium speed. Only use as much milk as is necessary to give the mixture a slow dropping consistency. Carefully stir in the currants and raisins and then transfer the mixture to a round greased cake tin 22-24 cm (9 inch) in diameter.

Oven temperatures

Conventional oven about 180°C/350°F (preheated)
Fan-assisted oven about 160°C/325°F (not preheated)
Gas oven mark 2–3 (not preheated)
Baking time 50–60 minutes.

Leave the cake in the tin for about 10 minutes, remove and then allow to cool fully.

For the icing (if required)

- 200 g (7 oz) icing sugar
- 30 g (2 tbsp) cocoa powder
- 3 tbsp hot water
- 25 g (1 oz) creamed coconut

Sift together the icing sugar and cocoa powder and add a little hot water, stirring to make a smooth, thick mixture. Melt the creamed coconut, stir into the icing and spread over the cooled cake.

Sand Cake
Sandkuchen

- 250 g (9 oz) margarine or butter
- 200 g (7 oz) sugar
- 2 tsp vanilla sugar
- 1 pinch salt
- a few drops of lemon essence

Melt the margarine or butter, pour into a mixing bowl and leave to cool. When cooled, use the whisk attachment on a hand mixer at high speed to cream the fat and the sugar, vanilla sugar, lemon essence and a pinch of salt, adding them gradually. Continue to beat until the mixture is light and fluffy.

(continued on page 28)

4 eggs	Add the eggs as you beat (one every 30 seconds or so). Sift together the flour, cornflour and baking powder. Add this to the creamed fat, beating continuously at medium speed.
125 g (4½ oz) plain flour	
125 g (4½ oz) cornflour	
½ tsp baking powder	Transfer the mixture to a greased 30 cm (12 inch) sponge tin 11 cm (4 inch) high, lined with non-stick baking paper.

Oven temperatures	
Conventional oven	160–180°C/325–350°F (preheated)
Fan-assisted oven	about 150°C/300°F (not preheated)
Gas oven	mark 2–3 (not preheated)
Baking time	65–75 minutes.
	Remove the cake from the tin and leave to cool.

Round Cake with Quark

Napfkuchen mit Quark

125 g (4½ oz) margarine or butter
6 tbsp vegetable oil
150 g (5½ oz) sugar
2 tsp vanilla sugar
5 drops butterscotch flavouring
1 pinch salt
2 eggs
250 g (9 oz) low-fat quark
375 g (13 oz) plain flour
15 g (1 tbsp) baking powder
5 tbsp milk
100 g (3½ oz) raisins
150 g (5½ oz) dried apricots, finely chopped
cake or biscuit crumbs

Use the whisk attachment on a hand mixer at high speed to cream the margarine or butter and then gradually add the oil, sugar, vanilla sugar, butterscotch flavouring and a pinch of salt. Continue to beat until the mixture is light and fluffy. Add the eggs as you beat (one every 30 seconds or so). Stir in the low-fat quark. Sift together the flour and baking powder. Add this and the milk to the creamed fat a little at a time, beating continuously at medium speed.

Carefully fold in the raisins and finely chopped dried apricots at medium speed.

Sprinkle cake or biscuit crumbs around the inside of the greased 22-24 cm (9 inch) sponge tin and then spoon in the mixture.

Oven temperatures	
Conventional oven	about 180°C/350°F (preheated)
Fan-assisted oven	about 180°C/325°F (not preheated)
Gas oven	mark 2–3 (not preheated)
Baking time	about 1 hour.
	Leave the cake to stand in the tin for about 10 minutes, remove,
30 g (1 oz) icing sugar	leave to cool further and then dust with icing sugar.

Waves of the Danube

for children

Donauwellen

For the mixture

250 g (9 oz) margarine or butter 200 g (7 oz) sugar 2 tsp vanilla sugar 1 pinch salt 5 eggs 375 g (13 oz) plain flour 3 tsp baking powder 4 tsp cocoa powder 1 tbsp milk about 700 g (1lb 9 oz) preserved sour cherries, pitted	Use the whisk attachment on a hand mixer at high speed to cream the margarine or butter and then gradually add the sugar, vanilla sugar and a pinch of salt. Continue to beat until the mixture is light and fluffy. Add the eggs as you beat (one every 30 seconds or so). Sift together the flour and baking powder. Add to the creamed fat a little at a time, beating at medium speed. Spread just under 2/3 of the mixture on to a greased baking tray. Sift the cocoa powder and then stir it into the rest of the mixture, together with the milk. Spread the chocolate-coloured mixture evenly over the lighter mix, fold a piece of aluminium foil several times and place it around the mixture. Drain the liquid from the sour cherries and arrange them evenly over the surface of the mixture.

Oven temperatures

Conventional oven	170–200°C/400°F (preheated)
Fan-assisted oven	150–170°C/350°F (not preheated)
Gas oven	mark 3–4 (preheated)
Baking time	35–40 minutes.
	Leave to cool.

For the buttercream

1 packet vanilla pudding powder 100 g (3½ oz) sugar 500 ml (18 fl oz) milk 250 g (9 oz) softened butter	Make the pudding with the sugar and milk according to the instructions. Leave to cool, stirring from time to time. Cream the butter and then stir it, a tablespoon at a time, into the cooled pudding. Make sure that neither the butter nor pudding gets too cold, or the mixture may curdle. Spread the buttercream evenly over the cake and leave in a cool place.

For the icing

200 g (7 oz) plain baking chocolate 4 tsp creamed coconut	Break up the plain chocolate and melt it with the creamed coconut over low heat in a bain-marie. Stir the mixture until it thickens. When the buttercream has set, spread the icing over the cake and make 'waves' on the surface with an icing comb or the tines of a fork.

Spring Cake

Frühlingstorte

for special occasions

	For the batter
250 g (9 oz) margarine or butter 250 g (9 oz) sugar 2 tsp vanilla sugar 5 eggs 250 g (9 oz) plain flour 2 tsp baking powder	Use the whisk attachment on a hand mixer at high speed to cream the margarine or butter, then gradually add the sugar and vanilla sugar. Continue to beat until the mixture is light and fluffy. Add the eggs as you beat (one every 30 seconds or so). Sift together the flour and baking powder. Add this to the creamed fat, beating at medium speed. Grease the base of a 26 cm (11 inch) springform tin and transfer the batter to it.
Oven temperatures	
Conventional oven	about 180°C/350°F (preheated)
Fan-assisted oven	about 160°C/325°F (not preheated)
Gas oven	mark 2–3 (not preheated)
Baking time	about 40 minutes. Remove the cake from the tin and leave to cool.
	For the filling
3 tbsp lemon juice 500 g (1lb 2 oz) low-fat quark 500 ml (18 fl oz) double cream 50 g (2 oz) sugar 15 g (1 tbsp) cream of tartar 4 tbsp redcurrant jelly	Stir the lemon juice into the low-fat quark. Whip the cream for about 30 seconds. Stir the sugar and cream of tartar into the cream and whip until stiff. Fold in the quark. Cut the cake twice crossways to make three sponge layers. Coat the bottom sponge layer with half of the redcurrant jelly and a third of the quark cream. Place the middle sponge layer on top and coat with the other half of the currant jelly and half of the remaining quark cream. Cover with the top sponge layer and then spread the surface and sides of the cake with the remaining quark cream.
about 50 g (2 oz) chopped pistachio nuts or blanched chopped and toasted almonds 2 tsp cocoa powder 2 tsp icing sugar, sifted	Sprinkle with chopped pistachio nuts or blanched, chopped and toasted almonds. Cut out 12 or 16 paper flowers from greaseproof paper to use as templates and lay them on the surface of the cake. Combine the cocoa powder and sifted icing sugar, shake over the surface and then carefully remove the paper.
Tip	This makes an ideal Easter Cake. You can decorate it with miniature chocolate eggs or fondant icing.

Snow Cake
Schneetorte

for guests

For the batter

100 g (3½ oz) margarine or butter 100 g (3½ oz) sugar 2 tsp vanilla sugar 1 pinch salt 4 egg yolks	Use the whisk attachment on a hand mixer at high speed to cream the margarine or butter and then gradually add the sugar, vanilla sugar and a pinch of salt. Continue to beat until the mixture is light and fluffy. Add the egg yolks as you beat (one just less than every 30 seconds).
125 g (4½ oz) plain flour ½ tsp baking powder	Sift together the flour and baking powder. Add this to the creamed fat, beating continuously at medium speed. Have two 28 cm (11 inch) greased springform tins ready.

For the meringue

4 egg whites 200 g (7 oz) caster sugar 100 g (3½ oz) blanched, chopped almonds	Beat the egg whites until stiff, then gradually add in the caster sugar. Spread half the batter on one of the springform tin base s and top with half the meringue. Sprinkle with half the blanched, chopped almonds. Bake each sponge layer in the springform tin with the surround fitted.
Oven temperatures	
Conventional oven	about 180°C/350°F (preheated)
Fan-assisted oven	about 160°C/325°F (not preheated)
Gas oven	mark 2-3 (preheated)
Baking time	bake each base for about 20 minutes. Immediately after baking, remove the sponge layers from the springform tins and cool them on wire racks.

For the filling

375–500 g (13oz-1lb 2 oz) canned gooseberries 1 packet clear jelly glaze 25 g (1 oz) sugar 500 ml (18 fl oz) double cream 15 g (1tbsp) cream of tartar 2 tsp sugar	Drain the gooseberries, reserving 250 ml (9 fl oz) of the juice. Follow the instructions for making the clear glaze, mixing the sugar with the reserved gooseberry juice. Stir in the gooseberries and leave to cool. Beat the double cream with the sugar and cream of tartar. Coat one sponge layer first with the gooseberry glaze and then with the whipped cream. Cut the other sponge layer into 16 slices and arrange on top of the cream.

Fruit Tart

Obsttorte

quick

For the mixture

- 100 g ($3\frac{1}{2}$ oz) margarine or butter
- 100 g ($3\frac{1}{2}$ oz) sugar
- 2 tsp vanilla sugar
- 1 pinch salt
- 2 eggs
- 100 g ($3\frac{1}{2}$ oz) plain flour
- 1 pinch baking powder

Use the whisk attachment on a hand mixer at high speed or a food processor to cream the margarine or butter and then gradually add the sugar, vanilla sugar and a pinch of salt. Continue to beat until the mixture is light and fluffy. Add the eggs as you beat (one every 30 seconds or so). Sift together the flour and baking powder. Add this and the milk to the creamed fat a little at a time, beating continuously at medium speed.

Transfer to a well greased 28 cm (11 inch) flan tin or greased tartlet tins and level off the surface.

Oven temperatures	
Conventional oven	170–200°C/350–400°F (preheated)
Fan-assisted oven	160–180°C/325–350°F (not preheated)
Gas oven	mark 3–4 (not preheated)
Baking time	20–25 minutes.

For the topping

- 1 kg (2lb 4 oz) berry fruits (strawberries, blackberries, raspberries, redcurrants, loganberries, blackcurrants, etc) fresh, preserved, stewed or canned
- sugar

Wash the berry fruits and leave to drain. Top and tail, remove skin and discard any that are imperfect. Halve or cut into slices. Sprinkle with sugar and leave for a short time.

If using stewed or bottled fruit, drain off any liquid.

Arrange the fruit on the cake.

For the glaze

- 1 packet jelly glaze
- sugar as required by jelly glaze
- 250 ml (9 fl oz) fruit juice or water

Follow the instructions on the jelly glaze packet, using fruit juice instead of water if preferred, and pour the glaze over the fruit. Refrigerate until set.

Heavenly Cake

Himmelstorte

for guests

	For the batter
250 g (9 oz) margarine or butter 200 g (7 oz) sugar 2 tsp vanilla sugar 1 pinch salt 5 egg yolks 250 g (9 oz) plain flour 2 tsp baking powder	Use the whisk attachment on a hand mixer at high speed or a food processor to cream the margarine or butter and then gradually add the sugar, vanilla sugar and the salt. Continue to beat until the mixture is light and fluffy. Add the egg yolks as you beat (one just under every 30 seconds). Sift together the flour and the baking powder. Add this to the creamed fat a little at a time, beating continuously at medium speed. Have four greased 28 cm (11 inch) springform tins ready.
	For the topping
5 egg whites 1 tbsp sugar	Whisk the egg whites until stiff and then stir in the sugar. To make four bases, spread 2 tablespoons of the cake mixture on each of the four greased springform tin bases. Ensure that the mixture is not too thin at the edges, otherwise it may burn slightly. Spoon a quarter of the whisked egg white on to each base.
40 g (1½ oz) sugar pinch ground cinnamon 100 g (3½ oz) blanched chopped almonds	Mix the sugar with the ground cinnamon and then sprinkle a quarter on each base. Similarly, sprinkle a quarter of the blanched, chopped almonds on each base. Without using the springform ring, bake each base until light brown.
Oven temperatures	
Conventional oven	170–200°C/350–400°F (preheated)
Fan-assisted oven	160–170°C/325°F (not preheated)
Gas oven	mark 3–4 (preheated)
Baking time	15–20 minutes.
	Remove the cake bases and springform base from the oven when baked and place on a cooling rack. Leave for about 20 minutes before removing from the springform base. Leave to cool completely before adding the filling.
	For the filling
500 g (1lb 2 oz) redcurrants 125 g (4 1/2 oz) sifted icing sugar 500 ml (18 fl oz) double cream 45 g (3 tbsp) cream of tartar	Wash and drain the redcurrants. Wipe them dry and sprinkle with sifted icing sugar. Whip the cream for 30 seconds. Add the cream stiffener, whip the cream until stiff and then fold in the redcurrants. Spread the filling over the bases and then place one on top of one another. The top layer should be a base.
Variation	You can use raspberries for the filling if you prefer, in which case only add 50 g (2 oz) icing sugar.

Prince Regent Cake

Prinzregententorte

for guests

For the cake batter

250 g (9 oz) margarine or butter 250 g (9 oz) sugar 2 tsp vanilla sugar 1 pinch salt 4 eggs 200 g (7 oz) plain flour 50 g (2 oz) cornflour 1 tsp baking powder	Use the whisk attachment on a hand mixer at high speed or a food processor to cream the margarine or butter and then gradually add the sugar, vanilla sugar and a pinch of salt. Continue to beat until the mixture is light and fluffy. Add the eggs as you beat (one every 30 seconds or so). Sift together the flour, cornflour and baking powder. Add this and the milk to the creamed fat a little at a time, beating continuously at medium speed. Make 8 sponge layers with this mixture To prepare one layer, spread 2 tablespoons of the cake mixture on a greased springform tin base about 28 cm (11 inch) in diameter lined with non-stick baking paper. Ensure that the edges are not too thin, otherwise they may burn slightly. Without using the springform surround, bake each layer until light brown.

Oven temperatures	
Conventional oven	170–200°C/350–400°F (preheated)
Fan-assisted oven	160–170 °C/325°F (not preheated)
Gas oven	mark 3–4 (preheated)
Baking time	bake each base for 8–10 minutes.

Remove the sponge layers from the springform base as soon as they come out of the oven and leave to cool on a cooling rack.

For the buttercream

1 packet chocolate pudding powder 100 g (3½ oz) sugar 500 ml (18 fl oz) milk 250 g (9 oz) butter	Follow the instructions for making the chocolate pudding, but use 100 g (3½ oz) sugar. Leave to cool, stirring from time to time. Cream the butter and then stir a tablespoon at a time into the cooled pudding. Make sure that neither the butter nor the pudding gets too cold, as curdling can occur. Spread the buttercream on seven of the sponge layers and then place one on top of the another. Top with the plain sponge layer.

For the icing

150 g (5½ oz) plain baking chocolate 25 g (1 oz) creamed coconut	Break the chocolate into pieces and melt, together with the creamed coconut, over a low heat in a bain-marie. Stir the mixture until it thickens. Spread the icing over the cake.

Tip Place some of the buttercream in a piping bag and decorate the top of the cake with swirls. Finish with chocolate buttons.

Sacher Torte

Sachertorte

traditional

For the mixture

160 g (6 oz) plain baking chocolate 160 g (6 oz) margarine or butter 160 g (6 oz) sugar 2 tsp vanilla sugar 6 egg yolks 100 g (3½ oz) cake or biscuit crumbs 6 egg whites	Break up the plain chocolate and melt over a low heat in a bain-marie. Stir the chocolate mixture until it thickens. Use the whisk attachment on a hand mixer at high speed or a food processor to cream the margarine or butter and then gradually add the sugar and vanilla sugar. Continue to beat until the mixture is light and fluffy. Add the egg yolks as you beat (one just under every 30 seconds). Beat the breadcrumbs and chocolate into the mixture at medium speed. Whisk and fold in the egg whites. Transfer the mixture to a greased 26 cm (10½ inch) springform tin lined with non-stick baking paper.

Oven temperatures

Conventional oven	about 170°C/360°F (preheated)
Fan-assisted oven	about 150°C/300°F (not preheated)
Gas oven	mark 2–3 (not preheated)
Baking time	about 45 minutes.

Remove the base from the tin, invert and leave to cool. Cut in half crossways (photo 1).

125 g (4½ oz) apricot jam	Spread the apricot jam on one half (photo 2) and cover with the other.

For the icing

2 tbsp sugar 3 tbsp water 100 g (3½ oz) plain baking chocolate	Heat the sugar with the water until it dissolves. Break the plain chocolate into small pieces. Add to the syrup and keep stirring until the icing looks shiny. Spread over the cooled cake. When the icing has set, cut the cake into slices (photo 3).

Serving suggestion Whipped cream.

Lemon and Quark Cream Cake

for guests

Zitronen-Quark-Sahnetorte

For the mixture

150 g (5½ oz) margarine or butter **150 g (5½ oz) sugar** **2 tsp vanilla sugar** **1 pinch salt** **3 eggs** **125 g (4¼ oz) plain flour** **25 g (1 oz) cornflour** **1 tsp baking powder**	Use the whisk attachment on a hand mixer at high speed to cream the margarine or butter and then gradually add the sugar, vanilla sugar and a pinch of salt. Continue to beat until the mixture is light and fluffy. Add the eggs as you beat (one every 30 seconds or so). Sift together the flour, the cornflour and baking powder. Add this to the creamed fat a little at a time, beating continuously at medium speed. Transfer to a 28 cm (11 inch) greased springform tin and level off the surface.

Oven temperatures	
Conventional oven	about 180°C/350°F (preheated)
Fan-assisted oven	about 160°C/325°F (not preheated)
Gas oven	mark 2–3 (not preheated)
Baking time	25–30 minutes.

Remove the base from the tin, leave to cool and cut in half horizontally to make two sponge layers.

For the filling

20 g (1 oz) unflavoured gelatine **8 tbsp cold water** **8 tbsp lemon juice** **150 g (5½ oz) sugar** **2 tsp vanilla sugar** **500 g (1 lb 2 oz) low-fat quark** **500 g (1 lb 2 oz) cream cheese** **1 untreated lemon, rind grated** **500 ml (18 fl oz) double cream**	Mix the gelatine and cold water and leave to stand for about 10 minutes. Line the springform tin with non-stick baking paper. Beat together the lemon juice, sugar and vanilla sugar until creamy. Stir in the low-fat quark, cream cheese and grated lemon rind. Heat the gelatine and stir until it has dissolved. Mix first with a couple of tablespoons of the quark mixture and then this add to the remainder. Whip the cream until stiff and stir it into the quark mixture. Return the lower sponge layer to the springform base. Place the ring surround around the cake base and cover the lower sponge layer with the quark filling. Level off the surface with a spatula. Cut the top sponge layer into 16 pieces and arrange them on the filling. Leave to set.
4 tbsp icing sugar	Remove the ring surround and dust with icing sugar before serving.

Truffle Cake Bars

for guests

Trüffelkuchen auf dem Blech

For the mixture

- 200 g (7 oz) margarine or butter
- 200 g (7oz) sugar
- 2 tsp vanilla sugar
- 1 pinch salt
- 4 eggs
- 200 g (7 oz) plain flour
- 4 tsp cocoa powder
- 1 tsp baking powder
- 3 tbsp milk

Use the whisk attachment on a hand mixer at high speed or a food processor to cream the margarine or butter and then gradually add the sugar, vanilla sugar and a pinch of salt. Continue to beat until the mixture is light and fluffy. Add the eggs as you beat (one every 30 seconds or so). Sift together the flour, cocoa powder and baking powder. Add this and the milk to the creamed fat a little at a time, beating continuously at medium speed.
Spread the mixture on to a greased Swiss roll tin, lined with non-stick baking paper. Fold up the paper around the edges of the tin.

Oven temperatures

Conventional oven	170–200°C/350–400°F (preheated)
Fan-assisted oven	160–170°C/325°F (not preheated)
Gas oven	mark 3–4 (preheated)
Baking time	about 15 minutes.

- 100 ml (3½ fl oz) orange juice

Invert the cake on to a sheet of non-stick baking paper as soon as it comes out of the oven. Pour the orange juice over it and leave to cool.

For the truffle cream

- 200 ml (7 fl oz) double cream
- 50 g (2 oz) butter
- 300 g (10 oz) plain baking chocolate
- 1-2 tbsp orange liqueur
- 100 g (3 ½ oz) white chocolate shavings

Bring the double cream and butter to the boil and remove from the heat.
Break the plain chocolate into pieces, stir into the hot cream and leave to dissolve. Leave in a cool place (preferably overnight).
Beat the chocolate cream with an electric whisk or about 2 minutes. Add the orange liqueur.
Spread the chocolate cream over the orange-soaked cake and decorate with an icing comb or fork.
Sprinkle with white chocolate shavings. Slice into bars.

Grilled Layer Cake

sophisticated

Grillkuchen (Schichtkuchen)

For the mixture

250 g (9 oz) margarine or butter
250 g (9 oz) sugar
2 tsp vanilla sugar
1 pinch salt
2 eggs
4 egg yolks
4 tbsp rum
150 g (5½ oz) plain flour
100 g (3½ oz) cornflour
3 tsp baking powder
4 egg whites

Use the whisk attachment on a hand mixer at high speed or a food processor to cream the margarine or butter and then gradually add the sugar, vanilla sugar and a pinch of salt. Continue to beat until the mixture is light and fluffy. Add the eggs and egg yolks as you beat (one every 30 seconds or so). Stir in the rum.
Sift together the flour, cornflour and baking powder. Add this to the creamed fat a little at a time, beating continuously at medium speed.
Whisk the egg whites until stiff and then carefully fold them into the mixture.
Place non-stick baking paper on the greased base of a 30 cm (12 inch) cake tin and then spread a generously heaped tablespoon of the mixture evenly over the base.
Place the tin under the preheated grill. There should be about 20 cm (8 inch) between the grill and cake mixture.
Grill until light brown.

Grilling time (gas or electric stove) Grill for about 2 minutes.

Spread the second layer (1-2 tablespoons) on top of the first and bake under the grill in the same way. Continue this process until all the cake mixture has been used up. Adjust the grill shelf height so that the distance between grill and uncooked cake mixture remains at around 20 cm (8 inch).
When the last layer has been cooked, carefully prise the cake away from the edge of the tin and turn out carefully on to a baking sheet. Remove the paper and then return the cake to a hot oven for about 5 minutes.

For the icing

100 g (3½ oz) plain chocolate
25 g (1 oz) creamed coconut

Break up the chocolate and melt it, together with the creamed coconut, over a low heat in a bain-marie. Stir the mixture until it thickens. When the cake has cooled, coat it with the chocolate icing.

Tip: Instead of one cake, make four bars. Cut the cake into four strips and ice each bar.

Frankfurt Garland Cake

traditional

Frankfurter Kranz

For the batter

- 100 g (3½ oz) margarine or butter
- 150 g (5½ oz) sugar
- 2 tsp vanilla sugar
- 4 drops lemon essence or
- ¼ tsp rum essence
- 1 pinch salt
- 3 eggs
- 150 g (5½ oz) plain flour
- 50 g (2 oz) cornflour
- 2 tsp baking powder

Use the whisk attachment on a hand mixer at high speed to cream the margarine or butter and then gradually add the sugar, vanilla sugar, lemon flavouring, rum essence and a pinch of salt. Continue to beat until the mixture is light and fluffy. Add the eggs as you beat (one every 30 seconds or so). Sift together the flour, cornflour and baking powder. Add this to the creamed fat a little at a time, beating continuously at medium speed.
Grease a deep ring mould, 20 cm (8 inch) in diameter and pour the batter into it.

Oven temperatures

Conventional oven about 180°C/350°F (preheated)
Fan-assisted oven about 160°C/325°F (not preheated)
Gas oven mark 2–3 (not preheated)
Baking time 35–45 minutes.

Leave the garland cake in the tin for about 10 minutes and then turn out carefully on to a wire cooling tray.

For the buttercream

- 1 packet vanilla pudding powder
- 100 g (3½ oz) sugar
- 500 ml (18 fl oz) milk
- 250 g (9 oz) butter

Follow the instructions for the vanilla pudding (but with 100 g (3½ oz) sugar). Leave to cool, stirring from time to time.
Cream the butter and then stir a tablespoon at a time into the cooled pudding . Make sure that neither the butter nor pudding gets too cold, as curdling can occur.

(continued on page 44)

For the praline

15 g (½ oz) butter 60 g (2¼ oz) sugar 125 g (4½ oz) blanched, chopped almonds	Melt the butter, add the sugar and blanched, chopped almonds, stirring well. Continue to cook until the almonds are light brown. Spoon on to aluminium foil and leave to cool.
red jam	Cut through the garland twice crossways (photo 1). Spread the red jam over the bottom layer (photo 2). Assemble the three layers of the garland cake in a buttercream sandwich, spread the buttercream over it (reserving a small quantity) and coat with the praline (photo 3). Decorate the surface with the reserved buttercream.
cherries or red jam	Use cherries or red jam for extra decoration. If possible, leave for a day before eating.

Delicious Chocolate Cake

Feine Schokoladentorte

For the sponge batter

150 g (5½ oz) margarine or butter 75 g (2¾ oz) sugar 2 tsp vanilla sugar 1 pinch salt 150 g (5½ oz) plain cooking chocolate, melted 2 eggs 4 egg yolks 150 g (5½ oz) plain flour 2 tsp cocoa powder 1 tsp baking powder	Use the whisk attachment on a hand mixer at high speed or a food processor to cream the margarine or butter and then gradually add the sugar, vanilla sugar, melted plain chocolate and a pinch of salt. Continue to beat until the mixture is light and fluffy. Add the eggs and egg yolks as you beat (one just less than every 30 seconds). Sift together the flour, cocoa powder and baking powder. Add this to the creamed fat a little at a time, beating continuously at medium speed.
4 egg whites 75 g (3 oz) sugar	Whisk the egg whites until they are stiff enough for a knife cut to remain visible. Gradually add the sugar and then fold the egg whites into the cake mixture. Transfer to a 28 cm (11 inch) springform tin lined with non-stick baking paper and level off the surface with a metal spatula.

Oven temperatures	
Conventional oven	about 180°C/350°F (preheated)
Fan-assisted oven	about 160°C/325°F (not preheated)
Gas oven	mark 2-3 (not preheated)
Baking time	about 40 minutes.

Remove the base from the surround and leave it on a rack to cool.

4-6 tbsp redcurrant jelly	Slice through it crossways and coat the bottom layer with redcurrant jelly and cover with the upper half. Spread jelly evenly over the surface and sides.

For the icing

100 g ($3\frac{1}{2}$ oz) plain baking chocolate
5 tbsp double cream

Break up the plain chocolate and melt it, together with the cream, over a low heat in a bain-marie. Stir the mixture until it thickens and then spread it over the cake.

Rhubarb Slices with Crème fraîche Topping

for guests

Rhabarberschnitten mit Crème-fraîche-Guß

For the batter

250 g (9 oz) margarine or butter
250 g (9 oz) sugar
2 tsp vanilla sugar
$\frac{1}{4}$ tsp butterscotch flavouring
4 eggs
250 g (9 oz) plain flour
2 tsp baking powder
plain flour

Use the whisk attachment on a hand mixer at high speed to cream the margarine or butter and then gradually add the sugar, vanilla sugar and butterscotch flavouring. Continue to beat until the mixture is light and fluffy. Add the eggs as you beat (one every 30 seconds or so). Sift together the flour and baking powder. Add this to the creamed fat in two portions, beating continuously at medium speed.
Spread on to a greased baking sheet sprinkled with flour and level off the surface.

For the rhubarb topping

600 g (1 lb 5 oz) rhubarb

Wash the ready-weighed rhubarb without stripping the outer skin. Strip off the coarse skin, cut into 2 cm (1 inch)-long chunks and scatter over the batter.

Oven temperatures
Conventional oven 180–200°C/350–375°F (preheated)
Fan-assisted oven 160–180°C/325–350°F (not preheated)
Gas oven mark 3–4 (preheated)
Baking time about 30 minutes.

For the cream topping

2 packets butterscotch pudding mixture
80 g (3 oz) sugar
700 ml ($1\frac{1}{4}$ pints) milk
450 ml (16 fl oz) crème fraîche

Follow the instructions on the butterscotch pudding packages, adding the sugar but using only 700 ml (milk not 1 litre). Stir the crème fraîche into the still warm pudding . When the cake has baked for 30 minutes, cover the surface with the creamy mixture and cook for a further 15 minutes.

American iced buns

Amerikaner

for children

For the mixture

65 g (2½ oz) margarine or butter 90 g (3¼ oz) sugar 2 tsp vanilla sugar 5 drops butterscotch flavouring 1 pinch salt 2 eggs 250 g (9 oz) plain flour 3 tsp baking powder 100 ml (3½ fl oz) milk	Use the whisk attachment on a hand mixer at high speed to cream the margarine or butter and then gradually add the sugar, vanilla sugar, butterscotch flavouring and a pinch of salt. Continue to beat until the mixture is light and fluffy. Add the eggs as you beat (one every 30 seconds or so). Sift together the flour and baking powder. Add this and the milk to the creamed fat a little at a time, beating continuously at medium speed. With two tablespoons drop 12 even-sized spoonfuls of the mixture on to a baking sheet lined with non-stick baking paper (not too close together). Shape with a wet knife.
Oven temperatures	
Conventional oven	170–200°C/350–400°F (preheated)
Fan-assisted oven	about 160°C/325°F (not preheated)
Gas oven	mark 3–4 (preheated)
Baking time	20–25 minutes.
milk	Brush the surface of the buns with milk after about 15 minutes.

For the icing

200 g (7 oz) icing sugar 2-3 tbsp lemon juice chopped almonds chopped pistachio nuts sugar crystals shredded or grated coconut for sprinkling, or	Sift the icing sugar. Add the lemon juice and beat until thick. Spread the icing over the buns while they are still hot. Sprinkle with blanched, chopped almonds, chopped pistachios, sugar crystals or coconut flakes.
125 g (4 oz) chocolate cake covering 25 g (1 oz) creamed coconut	Alternatively, melt chocolate cake covering with creamed coconut over a low heat in a bain-marie. Stir the mixture until it thickens. Spread over the buns and decorate in any way you like.

Spice Cake

Gewürzkuchen

sophisticated

250 g (9 oz) margarine or butter 250 g (9 oz) sugar 2 tsp vanilla-sugar 5 drops almond essence 1 tsp ground cinnamon 1 pinch each ground cloves, nutmeg and cardamom 1 pinch salt 5 eggs 250 g (9 oz) plain flour 10 g (¼ oz) cocoa powder 1 tsp baking powder 125 g (4½ oz) blanched, ground almonds	Use the whisk attachment on a hand mixer at high speed or a food processor to cream the margarine or butter and then gradually add the sugar, vanilla sugar, almond essence, ground cinnamon, ground cloves, nutmeg and cardamom and a pinch of salt. Continue to beat until the mixture is light and fluffy. Add the eggs as you beat (one every 30 seconds or so). Sift together the flour, cocoa powder and baking powder. Add this to the creamed fat a little at a time, beating continuously at medium speed. Stir in the blanched, ground almonds at medium speed. Transfer to a greased 30 x 11 cm (12 x 4½ inch) cake tin.
Oven temperatures	
Conventional oven	about 180°C/350°F (preheated)
Fan-assisted oven	about 160°C/325°F (not preheated)
Gas oven	mark 2-3 (not preheated)
Baking time	about 45 minutes. Remove the cake from the tin and turn out carefully on to a wire rack.
30 g (1 oz) icing sugar	Dust with icing sugar.

Pineapple Marzipan Cake

Ananas-Marzipan-Kuchen

	For the mixture
200 g (7 oz) marzipan 175 g (6 oz) margarine or butter 175 g (6 oz) sugar 2 tsp vanilla sugar 1 pinch salt 3 eggs 300 g (10½ oz) plain flour 2 tsp baking powder 3 canned pineapple slices (about 200 g (7 oz))	Beat the marzipan well with the hand mixer and then add the margarine or butter, beating at high speed until smooth. Gradually add the sugar, vanilla sugar and a pinch of salt and continue to beat until the mixture is light and fluffy. Add the eggs as you beat (one every 30 seconds or so). Sift together the flour and baking powder. Add this to the creamed fat a little at a time, beating continuously at medium speed. Drain the juice from the canned pineapple and cut the fruit into small pieces. Stir them carefully into the mixture at medium speed and then transfer to a greased 30 cm (12 inch) cake tin lined with non-stick baking paper.

Oven temperatures	
Conventional oven	about 180°C/350°F (preheated)
Fan-assisted oven	about 160°C/325°F (not preheated)
Gas oven	mark 2–3 (not preheated)
Baking time	60–70 minutes.

Turn out the cake and leave to cool.

For the icing

100 g (3½ oz) semi-sweet baking chocolate
25 g (1 oz) creamed coconut

Break up the plain chocolate and melt it, together with the creamed coconut, over a low heat in a bain-marie. Stir the mixture until it thickens. When the cake has cooled, coat it with the icing.

Peach slices

popular

Pfirsichschnitten

For the mixture

150 g (5½ oz) margarine or butter
150 g (5½) sugar
2 tsp vanilla sugar
1 pinch salt
5 drops lemon essence
4 eggs
250 g (9 oz) plain flour
3 tsp baking powder

Use the whisk attachment on a hand mixer at high speed to cream the margarine or butter and then gradually add the sugar, vanilla sugar, lemon flavouring and a pinch of salt. Continue to beat until the mixture is light and fluffy. Add the eggs as you beat (one every 30 seconds or so). Sift together the flour and baking powder. Add this to the creamed fat in two halves, beating continuously at medium speed.
Transfer to a greased baking sheet, level off the surface and then place a piece of folded aluminium foil around the mixture.

For the topping

900 g (2 lb) canned peaches
150 g (5½ oz) plain flour
75 g (3 oz) sugar
2 tsp vanilla sugar
100 g (3½ oz) butter

Drain the canned peaches, cut them into slices and lay them on the cake mixture. In a bowl, mix together the flour, sugar and vanilla sugar. Add the butter in knobs and rub into the flour by hand or with two forks. Spread the crumble mixture over the peaches.

Oven temperatures	
Conventional oven	170–200°C/350–400°F (preheated)
Fan-assisted oven	160–180°C/325–350°F (not preheated)
Gas oven	mark 3–4 (preheated)
Baking time	about 25 minutes.

Slice the cake as required.

Tip: You could coat the peach slices with a lemon jelly glaze.

Wafer I

Eiserkuchen I

for special occasions

125 g (4 oz) butter
250 g (9 oz) sugar
2 tsp vanilla sugar
2 eggs
250 g (9 oz) plain flour
500 ml (18 fl oz) milk
bacon fat or vegetable oil

Melt the butter, pour it into a mixing bowl and leave to cool. Add the sugar and vanilla sugar to the slightly firm butter and beat with a hand mixer until the butter and sugar are fluffy.
Add the eggs as you beat. Sift the flour and add it to the creamed butter mixture. Add the milk a little at a time (photo 1).
Spoon a few tablespoons into a well-heated wafer iron, greased with either bacon fat or a little cooking oil (photo 2) and bake until golden brown.
Remove the wafer from the wafer iron and, while still hot, shape them into rolls or cornets (photo 3).
Store the wafer in a tin with a tight-fitting lid so that they stay crisp.

Topping or Filling

Stiffly whipped cream.

Wafer II

Eiserkuchen II

75 g (2¾ oz) margarine or butter
125 g (4½ oz) sugar
2 tsp vanilla sugar
1 egg
250 g (9 oz) plain flour
½ tsp ground cinnamon
325 ml (13 fl oz) lukewarm water

Use the whisk attachment on a hand mixer at high speed to cream the margarine or butter and then gradually add the sugar and vanilla sugar. Continue to beat until the mixture is light and fluffy. Add the egg as you beat. Sift together the flour and ground cinnamon and add this and the lukewarm water to the creamed fat a little at a time beating continuously at medium speed.
Leave to stand for 30 minutes.

Baking time and temperatures

Bake as above.

Crème Fraîche Waffles

quick

Crème-fraîche-Waffeln

300 ml (10 fl oz) crème fraîche
100 g (3½ oz) sugar
2 tsp vanilla sugar
grated rind of ½ unwaxed lemon
1 pinch salt
3 eggs
250 g (9 oz) plain flour
1 tsp baking powder
bacon fat or vegetable oil

Use the whisk attachment on a hand mixer at high speed to beat the crème fraîche. Add the sugar, vanilla sugar, grated lemon rind and a pinch of salt. Continue to beat until the mixture is light and fluffy. Add the eggs as you beat (one every 30 seconds or so). Sift together the flour and baking powder. Add this to the cream a little at a time, beating continuously at medium speed.
Heat a waffle iron and grease it with bacon fat or vegetable oil. Spoon 3 tablespoons or so of the batter on the greased waffle iron. Bake the waffles until golden brown. Turn them out on to a rack and leave to cool.

Serving suggestion

Serve with whipped cream, vanilla ice-cream, glacé berry fruits, fruit purée or fruit jelly.

Sand Waffles

easy

Sandwaffeln

175 g (6 oz) creamed coconut
175 g (6 oz) sugar
2 tsp vanilla sugar
¼ tsp rum essence
1 pinch salt
4 eggs
225 g (8 oz) plain flour
25 g (1 oz) cornflour
½ tsp baking powder
bacon fat or vegetable oil
icing sugar

Melt the creamed coconut, pour into a mixing bowl and leave to cool. Allow the cream to harden slightly and then beat with the hand mixer at high speed. Gradually add the sugar, vanilla sugar, rum flavouring and a pinch of salt. Continue to beat until the mixture is light and fluffy. Add the eggs as you beat (one every 30 seconds or so). Sift together the flour, cornflour and baking powder. Add this to the creamed fat a little at a time, beating continuously at medium speed.
Spoon 3 tablespoons or so of the batter into a well-heated waffle iron, greased with bacon fat or vegetable oil.
Bake the waffles until golden brown. Turn them out on to a cooling rack, leave to cool and dust with icing sugar.

Before you start baking

The butter or margarine must be soft and spreadable before it can be used with a hand mixer or in a food processor.

It is not usually necessary to grease baking sheets and tins when baking with sweet short-crust dough.
Fruit flan tins and tartlet tins are exceptions. Do not grease baking sheets when baking with biscuit doughs which have a high fat content.

The method

Mix the flour and baking powder and sift them into the mixing bowl.
The mixing and sifting process loosens up the grains and distributes the baking powder evenly throughout the flour. If cocoa powder is one of the ingredients, then this can also be added to the flour.

Do not sift wholemeal flour just mix it with the baking powder in a bowl.

Add all the other ingredients listed.
Always break an egg into a cup first to check that it is fresh. If any liquid is required, add it to the sugar or honey.
The baking fat — margarine or butter — should be soft and spreadable. Only when it is at the right temperature will the other ingredients blend in properly. If you use more flour than the recipe specifies, it may not all be absorbed, especially in the case of doughs with a high fat content. The dough will become crumbly and the pastry will be hard. If fruit is to be incorporated, always knead it in last of all.

Use the kneading hook on a food mixer, initially at low speed, then gradually increase to high speed as the dough firms up.

Only if the fat is soft and spreadable will the ingredients blend in properly, so always take the butter or margarine out of the refrigerator in good time.

Lightly dust the work surface with flour and then use both hands to knead the dough to a smooth texture.

Do not sprinkle too much flour on the work surface or the dough may become too dry and break up. Knead the dough rapidly with the flat of the hand.

Shape the dough into a roll.
If it has become sticky, place it in the refrigerator for a while or add some flour.

By shaping it into a roll, the dough can be rolled out more easily. You can prevent a high-fat dough from sticking by leaving it to chill. Only add flour to reduce stickiness if the dough includes water or milk.

Before rolling out the dough, make sure your work surface is clean, then dust it with an even coating of flour.

Rolling out the dough.
Roll out dough in fairly small pieces, so that it retains its texture while being rolled. This is particularly important when making small pastries. The rolling pin must rotate properly during the rolling out process and it must pass smoothly over the dough. Do not press too hard. While rolling out, occasionally slip a large palette knife under the dough to loosen it at any places which have stuck to the work surface.

When using pastry cutters, try to avoid wastage by collecting up offcuts. However, the quality of the dough does not improve if it is repeatedly kneaded and rolled out.

Bake pastry cases for fruit tarts either in a springform tin or in a greased flan tin. If using a springform tin, roll out two thirds of the dough on to the tin base. It may depend on the recipe, but normally you can knead the rest of the dough with another tablespoon of flour, shape it into a roll and press it around the edge of the dough base to make a 3 cm (1 inch) high rim. Press with two fingers against the tin. Finally, prick the dough base a few times with a fork to prevent air bubbles from forming.

Basic recipe
Grundrezept

150-200 g (5 ½ - 7 oz) plain flour
½-1 tsp baking powder
75-125 g (3-4½ oz) sugar
2 tsp vanilla sugar
1 pinch salt
1 egg
75–125 g (3-4½ oz) margarine or butter

Sift the flour and baking powder into the mixing bowl. Add the sugar, vanilla sugar, salt, egg and butter or margarine.
Use the kneading hook on a food mixer, initially at low speed, then gradually increase to high speed as the dough firms up. Dust the work surface with flour and knead the dough to a smooth texture. If it sticks, place it in the refrigerator for 20-30 minutes.
Roll out the dough on the base of a springform tin, a 38 x 28 cm (15 x 11 inch) Swiss roll tin or on a floured work surface. Shape the dough according to the recipe and bake.

Baking sweet shortcrust dough

Always follow the instructions when baking sweet shortcrust doughs. When dough is baked, remove it from the tin or sheet as soon as possible. Take pastry out of springform tins as soon as it comes out of the oven and then leave to cool.
Use a cooling rack, keeping small pastries well separated. Carefully remove biscuits from the baking sheet with a palette knife or spatula and spread them out to cool.

Fruit and Nut Tart

for children

Obst-Nuß-Torte (see photo on pages 54/55)

For the dough

150 g (5½ oz) plain flour 1 tsp baking powder 50 g (2 oz) sugar 2 tsp vanilla sugar 1 egg 75 g (3 oz) ground hazelnuts 100 g (3½ oz) margarine or butter	Sift the flour and baking powder into a mixing bowl. Add the sugar, vanilla sugar, egg, hazelnuts and margarine or butter. Use the kneading hook of the food mixer, initially at low speed, then gradually increase to high speed as the dough firms up. Dust the work surface with flour and knead the dough to a smooth texture. If it sticks, place it in the refrigerator for a while. Roll out the dough to form a circle about 29 cm (11½ inch) in diameter. Place it in a greased flan tin 28 cm (11 inch) in diameter and press down well to obtain a smooth surface. Prick the pastry here and there with a fork to prevent air bubbles from forming.

Oven temperatures

Conventional oven	170–200°C/350–400°F (preheated)
Fan-assisted oven	about 160°C/325°F (not preheated)
Gas oven	mark 3-4 (preheated)
Baking time	15–20 minutes.

Remove the pastry from the oven as soon as it is baked, turn out on to a rack and leave to cool.

For the topping

600-700 g (1lb 5 oz - 1lb 9 oz) berry fruits (strawberries, raspberries, blackberries, etc.) trimmed and washed	Arrange the berries on the pastry base.
3 tbsp blackberry jam 2 tbsp blanched, chopped almonds	Strain the jam through a sieve, bring it to the boil and reduce slightly, stirring well. Brush it over the fruit. Sprinkle the blanched, chopped almonds around the edge.
Serving with	Whipped cream.

Cherry and Cream Tartlets

for guests

Kirsch-Sahne-Törtchen

	For the dough
250 g (9 oz) plain flour 1 pinch baking powder 100 g (3 ½ oz) sugar 2 tsp vanilla sugar 1 pinch salt 1 egg yolk 175 g (6 oz) butter	Sift the flour and baking powder into a mixing bowl. Add the sugar, vanilla sugar, salt, egg yolk and butter. Use the food mixer's kneading hook, initially at low speed, then gradually increase to high speed as the dough firms up. Dust the work surface with flour and knead the dough to a smooth texture. If it sticks, place it in the refrigerator for a while. Roll out the dough thinly. Cut out circles with a crinkle-edged pastry cutter about 6 cm (2½ inch) in diameter and place them on the baking sheet.
1 egg white 1 tsp water 75 g (3 oz) coarse sugar crystals	Beat the egg white with a little water, brush half of the pastry circles with it and then sprinkle with sugar crystals.
	If you cannot find coarse sugar crystals use rainbow-coloured coffee sugar.
Oven temperatures	
Conventional oven	170–200°C/350–400°F (preheated)
Fan-assisted oven	160–170°C/325°F (not preheated)
Gas oven	mark 3–4 (preheated)
Baking time	about 10 minutes.
	For the filling
250 g (9 oz) canned morello cherries, stoned 400-500 ml (14-16 fl oz) double cream 4 tsp vanilla sugar 15 g (1 tbsp) cream of tartar	Drain the morello cherries. Whip the cream for 30 seconds. Mix together vanilla sugar and cream of tartar, add to the cream and whip until stiff. Pipe cream around the edge of the unsugared circles (underside), spoon the morello cherries into the middle and then place the sugared circles on top.

Linzer Torte

for special occasions

Linzer Torte

200 g (7 oz) plain flour
1 tsp baking powder
125 g (4 ½ oz) sugar
2 tsp vanilla sugar
2 drops almond essence
1 pinch ground cloves
1 tsp ground cinnamon
1 pinch salt
1 egg yolk
1 egg white
125 g (4 ½ oz) margarine or butter
125 g (4 ½ oz) unblanched, ground almonds
100 g (3½ oz) raspberry jam
1 tsp milk

Sift the flour and baking powder into a mixing bowl. Add the sugar, vanilla sugar, bitter almond flavouring, ground cloves, ground cinnamon, salt, half an egg yolk, egg white, margarine or butter, unblanched, ground almonds.
Use the food mixer's kneading hook, initially at low speed, then gradually increase to high speed as the dough firms up. Dust the work surface with flour and knead the dough to a smooth texture. Take just under half of the dough and roll it out into a circle the size of a 28 cm (11 inch) springform tin base and cut out between and 16 and 20 narrow strips. Roll out the rest of the dough on the springform tin base, cover with the raspberry jam, leaving about 1 cm (½ inch) uncovered around the edge. Lay the strips of dough over the jam in a lattice pattern. Beat the other half of the egg yolk with a little milk and brush on to the pastry strips.

Oven temperatures
Conventional oven 170–200°C/350–400°C (preheated)
Fan-assisted oven about 170°C/325°F (not preheated)
Gas oven mark 3–4 (not preheated)
Baking time 25–30 minutes.

Variation Double the ingredients. Roll out the dough on a baking sheet and coat with jam and dough lattice. Bake the cake as above and then cut into slices.

Tip The filling does not have to be raspberry jam. It could be stewed plums or blackcurrant jelly.

Silesian Poppyseed Tart

traditional

Schlesische Mohntorte

	For the dough
250 g (9 oz) plain flour 2 tsp baking powder 125 g (4½ oz) sugar 2 tsp vanilla sugar 1 pinch salt 1 egg 2 tbsp cold water 125 g (5½ oz) butter	Sift the flour and baking powder into a mixing bowl. Add the sugar, vanilla sugar, salt, egg, water and butter. Use the kneading hook on a food mixer, initially at low speed, then gradually increase to high speed as the dough firms up. Dust the work surface with flour and knead the dough to a smooth texture. Roll out at least half of the dough to cover the base of a 28 cm (11 inch) springform tin, shape the rest of the dough into a roll and arrange it around the edge of the dough base. Press it against the springform surround to make a rim about 3 cm (⅛ inch) high.
	For the topping
1 l (1¾ pints) milk 200 g (7 oz) semolina 200 g (7 oz) poppyseeds, freshly ground 200 g (7 oz) sugar 2 tsp vanilla sugar 150 g (5½ oz) butter 100 g (3½ oz) low-fat quark 2 eggs 50 g (2 oz) blanched, ground almonds 50 g (2 oz) raisins 2 tbsp rum	Bring the milk to the boil. Mix the semolina with the freshly ground poppy seeds, stir into the milk, leave to swell over a low heat and then remove. Stir in the sugar, vanilla sugar, butter, low-fat quark, eggs, blanched, ground almonds, raisins and rum.
1 pear	Peel, quarter, core and grate the pear and stir in well. Transfer the poppy seed mixture to the tin and level off thc surfacce.
Oven temperatures	
Conventional oven	about 180°C/350°F (preheated)
Fan-assisted oven	about 160°C/325°F (not preheated)
Gas oven	mark 3–4 (not preheated)
Baking time	about 1 hour.
Icing sugar	Dust with icing sugar.
Tip	Poppy seed tart tastes delicious served hot.

Friesian Crumble Cake

Friesische Streuseltorte

ideal for freezing

For the dough

- 250 g (9 oz) plain flour
- 1 pinch baking powder
- 4 tsp vanilla sugar
- 150 ml (5 fl oz) crème fraîche
- 175 g (6 oz) margarine or butter

Sift the flour and baking powder into a mixing bowl. Add vanilla sugar, crème fraîche and margarine or butter.
Use the kneading hook on a food mixer, initially at low speed, then gradually increase to high speed as the dough firms up. Dust the work surface with flour and knead the dough to a smooth texture. If it sticks, place it in the refrigerator for a while.
Divide the dough into four equal pieces.
Roll out each round of dough on the base of a 28 cm (11 inch) springform tin. Make sure the dough is not too thin at the edges or it will burn.
Prick the dough here and there with a fork to prevent air bubbles from forming. Fit the springform surround.

For the crumble

- 150 g (5 ½ oz) plain flour
- 75 g (2¾ oz) sugar
- 2 tsp vanilla sugar
- 1 pinch ground cinnamon
- 100 g (3½ oz) margarine or butter

Sift the flour into a mixing bowl. Add the sugar, vanilla sugar, ground cinnamon and finally the margarine or butter. Use the kneading hook on a hand mixer to knead the dough until it resembles coarse breadcrumbs. Cover the dough rounds evenly with the crumble (photo 1).

Oven temperatures

Conventional oven	200–220°C/400–425°F (preheated)
Fan-assisted oven	170–180°C/350°F (not preheated)
Gas oven	mark 3–4 (preheated)
Baking time	bake each base for about 15 minutes.

(continued on page 66)

Remove the dough rounds from the springform tins as soon as they come out of the oven. Cut one of the bases into 12 even slices. Arrange all the rounds and slices on wire racks to cool.

For the filling

500 ml (18 fl oz) double cream	Beat the cream for 30 seconds.
25 g (1 oz) sugar 15 g (1 tbsp) cream of tartar 2 tsp vanilla sugar 450 g (1 lb) stewed plums	Mix together the sugar, cream of tartar and vanilla sugar and whip until stiff. Spoon into a piping bag with a star nozzle. Spread a third of the stewed plums on to each of the three dough rounds. Pipe the whipped cream on top (photo 2). Assemble the three rounds with the 12 cut segments on top (photo 3).
icing sugar	Dust with icing sugar and chill.

Tip Cut the crumble with an electric knife before serving.

Creamy Cheesecake

Käsecremetorte

traditional

For the dough

150 g ($5\frac{1}{2}$ oz) plain flour 1 tsp baking powder 65 g ($2\frac{1}{4}$ oz) sugar 2 tsp vanilla sugar 2 egg yolks 1 tbsp water or milk 50 g (2 oz) margarine or butter	Sift the flour and baking powder into a mixing bowl. Add the sugar, vanilla sugar, egg yolks, water or milk and margarine or butter. Use the kneading hook on a food mixer, initially at low speed, then gradually increase to high speed as the dough firms up. Dust the work surface with flour and knead the dough to a smooth texture. Roll out two-thirds of the dough on to the greased base of a 26 cm ($10\frac{1}{2}$ inch) springform tin. Shape the rest of the dough into a roll and place around the edge of the dough base, pressing with two fingers against the tin surround to create a rim 3 cm ($1\frac{1}{4}$ inch) high.

Oven temperatures	
Conventional oven	about 200°C/400°F (preheated)
Fan-assisted oven	about 180°C/350°F (not preheated)
Gas oven	mark 3–4 (preheated)
Baking time	20–25 minutes.

For the topping

2 packets vanilla pudding powder 200 g (7 oz) sugar 500 ml (18 fl oz) milk ¼ tsp lemon essence 750 g (1 lb 10 oz) low-fat soft cheese 50 g (2 oz) raisins 3 egg whites 1 egg yolk 1 tbsp milk	Mix the pudding powder with two-thirds of the sugar and half the milk and stir. Bring all but one tablespoon of the rest of the milk to the boil, remove from the heat and add to the pudding mixture, stirring constantly. Bring to the boil and then remove from the heat. Add the lemon essence and the low-fat soft cheese. Return to the boil and remove from the heat. Pour into a bowl and stir in the raisins. Whisk the egg whites with the remaining sugar until stiff and fold into the cheese mixture. Spread over the pre-cooked base and level off the surface. Beat the egg yolk with the milk and brush it over the cheese mixture.
Oven temperatures	
Conventional oven	about 180°C/350°F (preheated)
Fan-assisted oven	about 160°C/325°F (not preheated)
Gas oven	mark 2–3 (not preheated)
Baking time	50–60 minutes. Use a knife to release the cake from the springform surround, but leave to cool in the tin.
Tip	Dust with icing sugar.
Variation	Instead of raisins, use drained, canned mandarin orange segments, or
370 g (12½ oz) canned sour cherries 1 packet red jelly glaze sugar (as per manufacturer's instructions) 250 ml (9 fl oz) cherry juice	drain the sour cherries and arrange on top of the cooled cake. Make up the jelly glaze according to the packet instructions, using 250 ml (9 fl oz) fruit juice and pour over the cherries.

Apple Pie Slices

Gedeckter Apfelkuchen auf dem Blech

suitable for freezing

For the dough

- 350 g (12 oz) plain flour
- 4 tsp baking powder
- 70 g (2½ oz) sugar
- 2 tsp vanilla sugar
- 1 egg
- 4 tbsp milk
- 150 g (5½ oz) margarine or butter

Sift the flour and baking powder into a mixing bowl. Add the sugar, vanilla sugar, egg, milk and margarine or butter.
Use the food mixer's kneading hook, initially at low speed, then gradually increase to high speed as the dough firms up. Dust the work surface with flour and knead the dough to a smooth texture. If it sticks, place it in the refrigerator for a while.
Roll out just under half the dough thinly for the dough cover. Cut out a 38 x 28 cm (15 x 11 inch) rectangle to fit a baking sheet the same size. Cover with non-stick baking paper to help roll it up (photo 1).
Roll out the rest of the dough on the greased baking sheet (photo 2).

For the filling

- 1 ½ kg (3 lb 5 oz) apples
- 50 g (2 oz) sugar
- 2 tsp vanilla sugar
- 1 pinch ground cinnamon
- 2 tbsp raisins
- 50 g (2 oz) butter
- about 50 g (2 oz) sugar

Peel, quarter, seed, and slice the apples and then stew gently with the sugar, vanilla sugar, ground cinnamon, raisins and butter. Leave to cool, adding sugar to taste.

(continued on page 70)

Spread the stewed apple over the dough base and unroll the remaining dough cover on top (photo 3).

1 egg yolk 1 tbsp milk 50 g (2 oz) blanched chopped almonds	Beat the egg yolk with a little milk and brush over the top of the pie. Sprinkle with blanched, chopped almonds. Prick the top with a fork in several places.
Oven temperatures	
Conventional oven	200–220°C/400–425°F (preheated)
Fan-assisted oven	180–200°C/350–400°F (not preheated)
Gas oven	mark 4–5 (preheated)
Baking time	20–25 minutes.

Variation Bake in a 26-cm (10½ inch) springform tin, halving the quantity of dough and filling.

Apple Crumble Cake

popular

Apfel-Streusel-Kuchen

For the dough

150 g (5½ oz) plain flour
1 pinch baking powder
100 g (3½ oz) sugar
2 tsp vanilla sugar
1 pinch salt
1 egg
100 g (3½ oz) margarine or butter

Sift the flour and baking powder into a mixing bowl. Add the sugar, vanilla sugar, salt, egg and margarine or butter.
Use the kneading hook of the food mixer, initially at low speed, then gradually increase to high speed as the dough firms up. Dust the work surface with flour and knead the dough to a smooth texture. If it sticks, chill it in the refrigerator for a while.
Roll out a good two-thirds of the dough on the base of a 28 cm (11 inch) springform tin and prick with a fork in several places. Place the springform surround around the base.

Oven temperatures	
Conventional oven	200–220°C/400–425°F (preheated)
Fan-assisted oven	about 180°C/350°F (not preheated)
Gas oven	mark 3–4 (preheated)
Baking time	about 10–12 minutes.

Remove from the oven and leave to cool.
Shape the rest of the dough into a roll. Place around the edge of the pre-cooked pastry base, pressing with two fingers against the tin surround to create a rim 2 cm (¾ inch) high.

	For the filling
about 1 1/2 kg (3 lb 5 oz) apples 75 g (3 oz) sugar 1 pinch ground cinnamon 75 g (3 oz) butter	Peel, quarter, core and chop the apples. Stew gently with the sugar, ground cinnamon and butter. Leave to cool slightly and then spread over the prebaked base.
	For the crumble
150 g (5½ oz) plain flour 100 g (3½ oz) sugar 2 tsp vanilla sugar 100 g (3½ oz) butter	Sift the flour and baking powder into a mixing bowl. Add the sugar, vanilla sugar and butter. Use the food mixer's kneading hook to work the mixture to a crumble with lumps of the required size. Spread evenly over the stewed apples.
Oven temperatures	
Conventional oven	200–220°C/400–425°F (preheated)
Fan-assisted oven	about 180°C/350°F (not preheated)
Gas oven	mark 3–4 (not preheated)
Baking time	about 40 minutes.
Tip	Use a cooking apple, such as a Bramley.
Serve with	Whipped cream.
Variation	**Cherry Crumble Cake**
	For the filling
1 kg (2 lb 4 oz) sour cherries 100 g (3½ oz) sugar 4 tsp cornflour about 1 tbsp sugar	Wash and drain the cherries, removing the stalks and stones. Mix with the sugar and leave for a short while to draw out the juices. Bring just to the boil and drain off the juice. When the juice and cherries have cooled, measure out 250 ml (9 fl oz) juice, topping up with water if necessary. Mix the cornflour with 4 tablespoons of the juice. Bring the rest of the juice to the boil. Remove from the heat and then stir in the thickened juice. Bring back to the boil for a moment, stir in the cherries and then leave to cool. Add sugar to taste and then spread over the prebaked base.

Russian Chip Cake

Russischer Zupfkuchen

traditional

For the dough

375 g (13 oz) plain flour	Sift the flour, cocoa powder and baking powder into a mixing bowl. Add the sugar, vanilla sugar, egg and margarine or butter. Use the kneading hook, on the food mixer initially at low speed, then gradually increase to high speed as the dough firms up. Dust the work surface with flour and knead the dough to a smooth texture. If it sticks, chill it in the refrigerator for a while.
40 g (1½ oz) cocoa powder	
3 tsp baking powder	
200 g (7 oz) sugar	
2 tsp vanilla sugar	
1 egg	
200 g (7 oz) margarine or butter	Roll out half the dough to cover the base of a 28 cm (11 inch) springform tin.

For the filling

500 g (1 lb 2 oz) low-fat soft cheese	Blend the low-fat soft cheese, the sugar, vanilla sugar, eggs, vanilla pudding powder and melted, cooled margarine or butter until smooth. Spoon into the tin and level off the surface.
200 g (7 oz) sugar	
2 tsp vanilla sugar	
3 eggs	
1 packet vanilla pudding powder	Chop the remaining pastry into little 'chips' and arrange over the filling.
250 g (9 oz) margarine or butter, melted and cooled	

Oven temperatures

Conventional oven	about 170°C/325°F (preheated)
Fan-assisted oven	about 150°C/300°F (not preheated)
Gas oven	mark 3–4 (not preheated)
Baking time	60–70 minutes.

Fruit Tartlets

Obsttörtchen (12-14)

simple

	For the dough
200 g (7 oz) plain flour 1 tsp baking powder 75 g (3 oz) sugar 2 tsp vanilla sugar 1 pinch salt 4 drops lemon essence 2 tbsp water 100 g (3½ oz) margarine or butter	Sift the flour and baking powder into a mixing bowl. Add the sugar, vanilla sugar, salt, lemon essence, water and margarine or butter. Use the kneading hook on the food mixer, initially at low speed, then gradually increase to high speed as the dough firms up. Dust the work surface with flour and knead the dough to a smooth texture. If it sticks, chill it in the refrigerator for 20-30 minutes. Roll out the dough thinly and then cut into circles using a round pastry cutter about 10 cm (4 inch) in diameter. Place in well-greased 10 cm (4 inch) tartlet tins and then prick with a fork in several places to prevent bubbles forming.
Oven temperatures	
Conventional oven	170–200°C/350–400°F (preheated)
Fan-assisted oven	160–170°C/325°F (not preheated)
Gas oven	mark 3–4 (preheated)
Baking time	10–15 minutes.
pinch cream of tartar	Release the pastry from the tins as soon as they come out of the oven, leave to cool and then sprinkle with a pinch of cream of tartar, to prevent the fruit from soaking into the pastry.
	For the filling
500-750 g (1 lb 2 oz-1 lb 10 oz) raw fruit (strawberries, raspberries, bilberries or grapes) sugar	Wash the raw fruit, drain well and remove the stalks. Sprinkle with sugar and leave to stand for about 20 minutes,
	or
stewed or canned fruit (apricots,peaches, cherries, gooseberries, mandarin oranges)	drain the stewed or bottled fruit, reserving the liquid for the jelly glaze, and arrange the fruit on the pastry bases.
	For the glaze
1 packet jelly glaze sugar as directed on the packet 250 ml (9 fl oz) water or fruit juice	Make the glaze according to the instructions on the packet with water or fruit juice and spread over the fruit.

	For decoration
250 ml (9 fl oz) double cream	Whip the cream for 30 seconds.
15 g (1 tbsp) cream of tartar	Mix the cream of tartar with vanilla sugar and add to the cream.
2 tsp vanilla sugar	Whip until stiff and then decorate the tartlets.

Multi-coloured Fruit cake

simple

Bunter Obstkuchen

	For the dough
250 g (9 oz) plain flour 1 tsp baking powder 75 g (3 oz) sugar 2 tsp vanilla sugar 1 egg 125 g (4½ oz) margarine or butter	Sift the flour and baking powder into a mixing bowl. Add the sugar, vanilla sugar, egg and margarine or butter. Use the kneading hook on a food mixer, initially at low speed, then gradually increase to high speed as the dough firms up. Dust the work surface with flour and knead the dough to a smooth texture. If it sticks, chill it in the refrigerator for a while. Roll out the dough on a baking sheet.
	For the topping
350 g (12 oz) canned sour cherries 240 g (8 oz) canned apricot halves 300 g (10½ oz) blanched, ground almonds 150 g (5½ oz) sugar 2 tsp vanilla sugar 2 eggs 250 ml (9 fl oz) double cream	Drain the cherries and apricot halves (canned) separately. Mix together the blanched, ground almonds, sugar, vanilla sugar, eggs and double cream and spread this over the pastry. Arrange the fruit on the almond cream in separate sections.
Oven temperatures	
Conventional oven	about 180°C/350°F (preheated)
Fan-assisted oven	about 160°C/325°F (not preheated)
Gas oven	mark 2–3 (preheated)
Baking time	35–45 minutes.
	For the apricot syrup
2 tbsp apricot jam 1 tbsp water	Press the apricot jam through a sieve. Mix with water and bring to the boil, stirring constantly. Brush over the still warm fruit.

Bilberry or Blueberry Slices

Heidelbeerkuchen vom Blech

for guests

For the dough

300 g (11 oz) plain flour
2 tsp baking powder
100 g (3½ oz) sugar
2 tsp vanilla sugar
2 eggs
100 g (3½ oz) butter

Sift the flour and baking powder into a mixing bowl. Add the sugar, vanilla sugar, eggs and butter.
Use the food mixer's kneading hook, initially at low speed, then gradually increase to high speed as the dough firms up. Dust the work surface with flour and knead the dough to a smooth texture. If it sticks, place it in the refrigerator for a while.
Roll out the dough on a greased baking sheet and bake until golden brown.

Oven temperatures

Conventional oven	170–200°C/350–400°F (preheated)
Fan-assisted oven	160–180°C/325–350°F (not preheated)
Gas oven	mark 3–4 (preheated)
Baking time	about 15 minutes.

For the topping

400 g (14 oz) double cream cheese (such as mascarpone)
1 tsp lemon or citron peel, finely chopped
125 g (4½ oz) sugar
4 tsp vanilla sugar
3 tsp custard powder
250 ml (9 fl oz) double cream
400 g (14 oz) bilberries or blueberries

Blend the double cream cheese with the pack of lemon peel, sugar, vanilla sugar and the custard powder. Whip the cream until stiff and fold into the cream mixture.

Pick over the bilberries or blueberries, wash, drain well and stir in carefully. Transfer on to the prebaked pastry base and return to the oven

Oven temperatures

Conventional oven	about 180°C/350°F (preheated)
Fan-assisted oven	about 160°C/325°F (not preheated)
Gas oven	mark 2–3 (preheated)
Baking time	about 25 minutes.

Tip If you prefer, you can use frozen bilberries or blueberries. Thaw the berries until they separate and can be stirred into the cream mixture.

Cheesecake with Crumble Topping

popular

Käsekuchen mit Streuseln

	For the dough
150 g (5½ oz) plain flour ½ tsp baking powder 75 g (3 oz) sugar 2 tsp vanilla sugar 1 pinch salt 1 egg 75 g (3 oz) margarine or butter 1 tbsp plain flour	Sift the flour and the baking powder into a mixing bowl. Add the sugar, vanilla sugar, salt, egg and margarine or butter. Use the food mixer's kneading hook, initially at low speed, then gradually increase to high speed as the dough firms up. Dust the work surface with flour and knead the dough to a smooth texture. If it sticks, place it in the refrigerator for a while. Roll out two-thirds of the dough on the base of a 28 cm (11 inch) springform tin. Knead tablespoon of flour into the rest of the dough and shape into a roll. Then press against the tin surround to create a 3 cm (1 inch) rim. Finally, prick the dough here and there with a fork to prevent air bubbles from forming.
Oven temperatures	
Conventional oven	200–220°C/400–425°F (preheated)
Fan-assisted oven	180–200°C/350–400°F (not preheated)
Gas oven	mark 3–4 (preheated)
Baking time	about 10 minutes.
	For the filling
750 g (1 lb 10 oz) low-fat soft cheese 150 g (5½ oz) sugar 3 tbsp lemon juice 50 g (2 oz) cornflour 3 egg yolks 3 egg whites 250 ml (9 fl oz) double cream	Mix the low-fat soft cheese with the sugar, lemon juice,cornflour and egg yolks. Whisk the three egg whites until stiff. Whip the cream until stiff. Fold both into the cream cheese mixture and spread evenly over the base.
	For the crumble
100 g (3½ oz) plain flour 75 g (3 oz) sugar 2 tsp vanilla sugar 75 g (3 oz) butter	Sift the flour into a mixing bowl and add the sugar, vanilla sugar and butter. Using the hand mixer's kneading hook to make the crumble and spread evenly over the filling.
Oven temperatures	
Conventional oven	about 170°C/325°F (preheated)
Fan-assisted oven	about 150°C/300°F (not preheated)
Gas oven	mark 2–3 (not preheated)
Baking time	70–80 minutes. When the cheesecake is baked, leave it in the oven with the door ajar for a further 15 minutes.

Poppy Seed Cheesecake

traditional

Mohn-Quark-Kuchen

For the dough

375 g (13 oz) plain flour
1 tsp baking powder
75 g (3 oz) sugar
2 tsp vanilla sugar
2 eggs
175 g (6 oz) margarine or butter

Sift the flour and baking powder into a mixing bowl. Add the sugar, vanilla sugar, eggs and the margarine or butter.
Use the food mixer's kneading hook, initially at low speed, then gradually increase to high speed as the dough firms up. Dust the work surface with flour and knead the dough to a smooth texture. If it sticks, chill it in the refrigerator for a while.

For the cream cheese layer

750 g (1 lb 10 oz) low-fat soft cheese
150 g (5½ oz) sugar
2 egg yolks
1 pinch salt
grated rind of ½ untreated lemon
60 g (2½ oz) cornflour
75 g (3 oz) melted butter
2 egg whites

Mix together the low-fat soft cheese, sugar, egg yolks, salt, grated lemon rind, cornflour and melted butter. Whisk the egg whites until stiff and then fold into the cream cheese mixture.

For the poppy seed layer

250 g (9 oz) poppyseeds
2 tbsp honey
2 eggs
100 g (3½ oz) sultanas

Grind the poppyseeds and cook with the honey, eggs and sultanas.

Roll out two-thirds of the dough on a 38 x 28 cm (15 x 11 inch) baking sheet. First spread the cream cheese mixture on top, followed by the poppyseed. Roll out the rest of the dough thinly and cut out strips about 1 cm (½ inch). Lay the strips on top of the poppy seed in a lattice pattern.

Oven temperatures

Conventional oven	170–200°C/350–400°F (preheated)
Fan-assisted oven	about 160°C/325°F (not preheated)
Gas oven	mark 3–4 (not preheated)
Baking time	about 50 minutes.

For the apricot syrup

3-4 tbsp apricot jam
3 tbsp water

Strain the apricot jam through a sieve. Mix with water and bring to the boil, stirring constantly. Brush it over the dough strips.

Nut or Coconut Triangles

popular

Nuß- oder Kokosecken

For the dough

150 g (5½ oz) plain flour	Sift the flour and baking powder into a mixing bowl. Add the
½ tsp baking powder	sugar, vanilla sugar, salt, egg and margarine.
65 g (2¼ oz) sugar	Use the kneading hook on the food mixer, initially at low speed,
2 tsp vanilla sugar	then gradually increase to high speed as the dough firms up. Dust
1 pinch salt	the work surface with flour and knead the dough to a smooth tex-
1 egg	ture. If it sticks, place it in the refrigerator for a while.
65 g (2¼ oz) margarine	Roll out the dough into a rectangle 32 x 24 cm (13 x 9½ inch) on a
2 tbsp apricot jam	baking sheet and brush with the apricot jam.

For the topping

100 g (3½ oz) margarine or butter	Slowly warm the margarine or butter, sugar, vanilla sugar and
100 g (3½ oz) sugar	water until the butter has melted. Stir in the ground hazelnuts and
2 tsp vanilla sugar	chopped hazelnuts or dessicated coconut. Leave to cool and then
2 tbsp water	spread evenly over the dough.
75 g (3 oz) ground hazelnuts	Fold a strip of aluminium foil several times and then place this
125 g (4½ oz) chopped hazelnuts	around the mixture, to hold it in place.
or	
200 g (7 oz) dessicated coconut	

Oven temperatures	
Conventional oven	180–200°C/350–400°F (preheated)
Fan-assisted oven	160–180°C/325–350°F (not preheated)
Gas oven	mark 3–4 (preheated)
Baking time	20–30 minutes.

Leave to cool. Cut into 8 x 8 cm (3¼ inch) squares and then halve diagonally.

For the icing

50 g (2 oz) chocolate cake covering	Mix the chocolate cake covering with the creamed coconut and
10 g (2 tsp) coconut cream	melt over a low heat in a bain-marie. Stir the mixture until it becomes smooth. Dip the two acute corners of the triangles into the icing.

Chocolate Cream Tartlets

for special occasions

Schokocremetörtchen (20 tartlets)

For the dough

- 250 g (9 oz) plain flour
- 50 g (2 oz) cornflour
- 1 tsp baking powder
- 50 g (2 oz) sugar
- 2 tsp vanilla sugar
- 30 ml (2 tbsp) sour cream or milk
- 175 g (6 oz) margarine or butter

Sift the flour and cornflour into a mixing bowl. Add the baking powder, sugar, vanilla sugar, sour cream or milk and margarine or butter.

Use the kneading hook of a food mixer, initially at low speed, then gradually increase to high speed as the dough firms up. Dust the work surface with flour and knead the dough to a smooth texture. If it sticks, chill it in the refrigerator for a while.

Roll out the dough to a thickness of about 3 mm (⅛ inch) and then cut out 40 or so circles, about 7 cm (2¾ inch) in diameter, using a crinkle cutter. Place on a baking sheet.

Oven temperatures

Conventional oven	170–200°C/350–400°F (preheated)
Fan-assisted oven	160–170°C/325°F (not preheated)
Gas oven	mark 3–4 (preheated)
Baking time	12–15 minutes.

For the buttercream

- 1 packet chocolate pudding powder
- 50 g (2 oz) sugar
- 4 tbsp milk
- 375 ml (13 fl oz) milk
- 150 g (5 ½ oz) butter
- 25 g (1 oz) coconut cream

Make the chocolate pudding according to the packet directions, using the quantities of sugar and milk given in this recipe and stirring occasionally as the mixture cools.

Soften the butter and then add to the cooled pudding a tablespoon at a time. Neither the butter nor the pudding should be too cold.

Melt the creamed coconut and stir into the mixture.

For the icing

- 100 g (3½ oz) plain chocolate cake covering
- 25 g (1 oz) coconut cream

Break the plain chocolate cake covering into pieces, add the creamed coconut and melt over a low heat in a bain-marie. Stir the mixture until it becomes smooth.

Brush half of the cooled biscuits with the chocolate icing and leave to set.

Pipe the buttercream on to the underside of the remaining biscuits. Place the chocolate-coated biscuits on top and decorate with a buttercream swirl.

Tip Prepare the tartlets the day before you intend to serve them.

Sweet Cheese Turnovers

Quarktaschen

For the dough

150 g (5½ oz) plain flour	Sift the flour into a mixing bowl. Add vanilla sugar, salt, low-fat soft cheese and margarine or butter.
2 tsp vanilla sugar	
1 pinch of salt	Use the food mixer's kneading hook, initially at low speed, then gradually increase to high speed as the dough firms up. Dust the work surface with flour and knead the dough to a smooth texture. Place it in the refrigerator for about an hour.
150 g (5½ oz) low-fat soft cheese	
150 g (5½ oz) margarine or butter	

For the filling

250 g (9 oz) low-fat soft cheese	Mix together the low-fat soft cheese, sugar, vanilla sugar, candied peel and the egg yolk.
50 g (2 oz) sugar	
2 tsp vanilla sugar	Whisk the egg white until stiff and fold in to the cheese mixture with the raisins.
1 tsp finely chopped candied citron or lemon peel	
1 egg yolk	Roll out half the dough into a 30 x 30 cm (12 x 12 inch) square, cut it into 10 x 10 cm (4 x 4 inch) squares and place a little of the cheese filling in the middle of each dough square.
1 egg white	
30 g (1 oz) raisins	
1 egg yolk	Beat the egg yolk with 1½ tablespoons of milk and brush around the edges of the dough squares.
1 1/2 tbsp milk	Fold each dough square over to make a turnover, place on a baking sheet lined with non-stick baking paper and brush with egg yolk. Roll out the rest of the dough and cut it into narrow strips. Arrange two dough strips on each turnover to make a cross and brush with egg yolk.

Oven temperatures	
Conventional oven	200–220°C/400–425°F (preheated)
Fan-assisted oven	about 180°C/350°F (not preheated)
Gas oven	mark 3–4 (preheated)
Baking time	about 25 minutes.

Almond Pastries

Zartes Mandelgebäck

simple

	For the dough
375 g (13 oz) plain flour 1 tsp baking powder 125 g (4½) oz sugar 2 tsp vanilla sugar 1 pinch salt 2 drops almond essence grated rind of 1 untreated lemon 1 egg 250 g (9 oz) margarine or butter 100 g (3½ oz) blanched, chopped almonds	Sift the flour and baking powder into a mixing bowl. Add the sugar, vanilla sugar, salt, almond essence, grated lemon rind, egg and margarine or butter. Use the kneading hook on a dough hook, initially at low speed, then gradually increase to high speed as the dough firms up. Add the blanched, slivered almonds and knead at medium speed for a short time. Dust the work surface with flour and knead the dough to a smooth texture. Roll out the dough into a 14 x 22 cm (5 ½ x 8 ½ inch) rectangle and leave in the refrigerator overnight to chill. Cut first into 22 x 3½ cm (8½ x 1½ inch) strips , then into fingers ½ to 1 cm (¼ to ½ inch) thick and arrange on a baking sheet.
Oven temperatures	
Conventional oven	170–200°C/350–400°F (preheated)
Fan-assisted oven	160–170°C/325°F (not preheated)
Gas oven	mark 3–4 (preheated)
Baking time	10-15 minutes.
	For the icing
175 g (6 oz) chocolate cake covering 25 g (1 oz) coconut cream	Break the chocolate cake covering into pieces, add the creamed coconut and melt over a low heat in a bain-marie. Stir the mixture until it becomes smooth. Dip a half of the cooled biscuits into the icing.

Heather Sand

Heidesand

traditional

250 g (9 oz) butter 200 g (7 oz) sugar 2 tsp vanilla sugar 1 pinch salt 2–3 tbsp milk	Melt the butter until it browns. Pour it into a mixing bowl and leave to cool. When the butter has reset, whisk at high speed until smooth. Gradually add the sugar, vanilla sugar, salt and milk and stir until the mixture becomes light and fluffy.

375 g (13 oz) plain flour 1 tsp baking powder	Sift the flour and baking powder into a mixing bowl and add two-thirds to the mixture a little at a time, beating at medium speed. Add the rest of the flour and knead to a smooth dough by hand on the work surface. Shape the dough into 3 cm (1¼ inch)-thick rolls and chill until they are hard. Cut the rolls into 5 mm (¼ inch)-thick slices and arrange on a baking sheet.
Oven temperatures	
Conventional oven	170–200°C/350–400°F (preheated)
Fan-assisted oven	160–170°C/325°F (not preheated)
Gas oven	mark 3–4 (preheated)
Baking time	10–15 minutes.

Wine Biscuits

Weinplätzchen

for guests

	For the dough
375 g (13 oz) plain flour 125 g (4½ oz) sugar 2 tsp vanilla sugar 3 tbsp white wine 200 g (7 oz) butter	Sift the flour into a mixing bowl. Add the sugar, vanilla sugar, white wine and butter. Use the kneading hook on a food mixer, initially at low speed, then gradually increase to high speed as the dough firms up. Dust the work surface with flour and knead the dough to a smooth texture. If it sticks, place it in the refrigerator for a while. Roll out the dough thinly in small portions. Cut out 4 cm (1½ inch) circles with a pastry cutter and arrange on a baking sheet.
	For the topping
2 egg whites 40 g (1½ oz) sugar a pinch ground cinnamon 50 g (2 oz) blanched, chopped almonds	Whisk the egg whites until they are stiff enough for a knife cut to remain visible and then brush over the dough circles. Mix the sugar and ground cinnamon and sprinkle over the biscuits, followed by the blanched, chopped almonds.
Oven temperatures	
Conventional oven	170–200°C/350–400°F (preheated)
Fan-assisted oven	160–170°C/325°F (not preheated)
Gas oven	mark 3–4 (preheated)
Baking time	10–15 minutes.
Tip	If there is insufficient almond topping for all the biscuits, sprinkle the remainder with the sugar and cinnamon mixture only.

Leipzig Larks

Leipziger Lerchen

traditional

For the dough

200 g (7 oz) plain flour ½ tsp baking powder 75 g (3 oz) sugar 2 tsp vanilla sugar 2 tbsp water 100 g (3½ oz) margarine or butter	Sift the flour and baking powder into a mixing bowl. Add the sugar, vanilla sugar, water and margarine or butter. Use the kneading hook on the food mixer, initially at low speed, then gradually increase to high speed as the dough firms up. Dust the work surface with flour and knead the dough to a smooth texture. If it sticks, chill it in the refrigerator for about 20 minutes. Roll out the dough thinly and cut out 12 circles (about 10 cm (4 inches) in diameter) (photo 1). Line 12 lightly greased moulds (about 4 cm (1½ inch) at the base, 8 cm (3¼ inch) at the top and 3-4 cm (1¼-1½inch) high) with the circles. Cut 12 small stars out of the remaining dough and put to one side.
100 g (3½ oz) apricot jam	Place 1 teaspoon apricot jam into each one (photo 2).

For the filling

80 g (3 oz) butter 125 g (4½ oz) sugar 1 egg 1 egg white 100 g (3½ oz) plain flour 125 g (4½ oz) blanched, ground almonds 2 drops almond essence 6 tbsp milk 2 tbsp rum 1 egg yolk	Whisk the butter with the hand mixer until smooth. Add the sugar, egg and egg white and stir well. Sift in the flour and then add the blanched ground almonds, almond essence, 5 tablespoons of the milk and rum. Spoon the mixture into the pastry moulds and top with the stars (photo 3). Beat the egg yolk with the remaining tablespoon of milk and brush the stars.

(continued on page 88)

Oven temperatures	
Conventional oven	180–200°C/400°F (preheated)
Fan-assisted oven	160–170°C/350°F (not preheated)
Gas oven	mark 3–4 (not preheated)
Baking time	about 25 minutes.
	Leave the pastries to cool for about 10 minutes and then remove from the moulds.

Hazelnut Garland

Haselnußkranz

sophisticated

For the dough

- 300 g (10½ oz) plain flour
- 2 tsp baking powder
- 100 g (3½ oz) sugar
- 2 tsp vanilla sugar
- 1 pinch salt
- 1 egg
- 2 tbsp milk or water
- 125 g (4½ oz) margarine or butter

Sift the flour and baking powder into a mixing bowl. Add the sugar, vanilla sugar, salt, egg, milk or water and margarine or butter.

Use the food mixer's kneading hook, initially at low speed, then gradually increase to high speed as the dough firms up. Dust the work surface with flour and knead the dough to a smooth texture. If it sticks, place it in the refrigerator for a while.

For the filling

- 200 g (7 oz) ground hazelnuts
- 100 g (3 ½ oz) sugar
- 4–5 drops almond essence
- 1 egg yolk
- 1 egg white
- 3-4 tbsp water
- 1 tbsp milk

Blend the ground hazelnuts with the sugar, almond essence, the half egg yolk, egg white and water until smooth.

Roll out the dough into a rectangle about 45 x 35 cm (18 x 14 inch) and spread the nut mixture on top. Roll the dough up from the long side and arrange in a garland shape on a greased baking sheet. Beat the other half of the egg yolk with the milk, brush over the garland and make star-shaped cuts in the surface.

Oven temperatures	
Conventional oven	170–200°C/350–400°F (preheated)
Fan-assisted oven	160–170°C/325°F (not preheated)
Gas oven	mark 3–4 (preheated)
Baking time	about 45 minutes.

Apricot Slices

popular

Aprikosenschnitten

	For the dough
250 g (9 oz) plain flour 2 tsp cocoa powder 1 tsp baking powder 100 g (3½ oz) sugar 2 tsp vanilla sugar 3 drops rum essence 200 g (7 oz) margarine or butter	Sift the flour, cocoa powder and baking powder into a mixing bowl. Add the sugar, vanilla sugar, rum flavouring and margarine or butter. Use the food mixer's kneading hook, initially at low speed, then gradually increase to high speed as the dough firms up. Dust the work surface with flour and knead the dough to a smooth texture. If it sticks, place it in the refrigerator for a while. Roll out the dough on to a 38 x 28 cm (15 x 11 inch) baking sheet and bake blind.
Oven temperatures	
Conventional oven	about 200°C/400°F (preheated)
Fan-assisted oven	about 170°C/350°F (not preheated)
Gas oven	mark 3–4 (preheated)
Baking time	about 12 minutes.
	For the topping
480 g (1 lb) canned apricot halves 2 egg whites 2 packets vanilla pudding powder 100 g (3½ oz) sugar 2 tsp vanilla sugar 2 egg yolks 750 ml (1¼ pints) milk 300 ml (5 fl oz) crème fraîche	Drain the canned apricot halves, reserving 250 ml (8 fl oz) juice. Whisk the egg whites until stiff. Following the instructions on the pack, prepare a vanilla-flavoured pudding pack, using the pudding powder, the sugar, vanilla sugar, egg yolks and 750 ml (1¼ pints) milk. When the mixture comes to the boil, fold in the crème fraîche and the whisked egg whites. Spread the mixture over the baked pastry base and wrap a folded strip of aluminium foil around the edge. Arrange the apricots on top of the cream, flat side down.
Oven temperatures	
Conventional oven	170–200°C/350–400°F (preheated)
Fan-assisted oven	about 160°C/325°F (not preheated)
Gas oven	mark 3–4 (preheated)
Baking time	30–35 minutes. Leave the pastries to cool.
	For the glaze
1 packet jelly glaze 25 g (1 oz) sugar 250 ml (9 fl oz) apricot juice	Follow the instructions on the clear glaze pack, using the sugar and the reserved apricot juice. Spread over the apricots and leave to set.

Cinnamon Leaves

Zimtblätter

simple

350 g (12 oz) plain flour
1 tsp baking powder
100 g (3½ oz) sifted icing sugar
2 tsp vanilla sugar
1 pinch salt
1 tsp ground cinnamon
3 egg yolks
250 g (9 oz) margarine or butter
300 g (10½ oz) blanched, coarsely ground almonds
1 tbsp honey
sugar mixed with ground cinnamon

For the dough

Sift the flour and baking powder into a mixing bowl. Add the sifted icing sugar, vanilla sugar, salt, ground cinnamon, 2 of the egg yolks, margarine or butter and blanched, coarsely ground almonds.

Use the kneading hook on a food mixer, initially at low speed, then gradually increase to high speed as the dough firms up. Dust the work surface with flour and knead the dough to a smooth texture. Place the dough in the refrigerator for 20-30 minutes.

Roll out the dough to a thickness of about 3 mm (⅛ inch). Use a ring-shaped pastry cutter to cut out oval leaf shapes (photo 1).

Arrange on a baking sheet lined with non-stick baking paper.

Beat the reserved egg yolk with the honey. Brush this over the leaf-shapes and sprinkle with sugar-and-cinnamon mixture (photo 2).

Oven temperatures

Conventional oven	170–200°C/350–400°F (preheated)
Fan-assisted oven	160–170°C/325°F (not preheated)
Gas oven	mark 3–4 (preheated)
Baking time	12–15 minutes.

125 g (5½ oz) chocolate cake covering
20 g (¾ oz) coconut cream

For the icing

Break the chocolate cake covering into small pieces and melt over a low heat in a bain-marie with the coconut cream. Stir the mixture until it becomes smooth. Coat the underside of the cooled biscuits with the mixture (photo 3).

You can use either dry yeast in a sachet or fresh yeast. The latter is available from some bakers and sometimes from health food shops. There are two types of dry yeast. Easyblend yeast is is sprinkled into the flour straight from the packet and dry yeast which must first be mixed with warm liquid. Do not use Easyblend yeast for cakes with a large number of ingredients, such as yeast pound cake or stollen, or any other cakes in which the yeast must be added to the liquid first.
Always use strong plain flour for yeast baking.

Method using Easyblend yeast

Sift the flour into a mixing bowl and distribute the dry yeast evenly throughout the flour with a fork.
Add all the remaining ingredients to the flour.
Yeast will only develop its full potential in the presence of warmth - the liquid, in particular, (milk or water) should be at about 37 °C/98.6°F (blood heat).

Then process the ingredients using the dough hook of a mixer, briefly at low speed and then at full speed for about 5 minutes.
The dough must be smooth.
Kneading the yeast dough binds the ingredients together particularly effectively, and also adds air to the mixture. In the process, the yeast converts the sugar and flour - the carbohydrates - into carbon dioxide and alcohol, causing the dough to rise.

Method using fresh or dry yeast mixed with liquid

In this case, the yeast needs to start to activate before it is mixed with the flour activate. The crumbled fresh yeast or dry yeast is combined with a little sugar or honey and lukewarm water or milk and left to stand at room temperature for 15 minutes. The yeast will only develop its full potential in the presence of warmth, so the liquid should be hand-hot, 37 °C/98.6°F .

The remaining ingredients must not be allowed to come into contact with the yeast while it is reacting with the flour. This applies in particular to salt and fat, which would prevent the yeast from causing the dough to rise. For this reason, these ingredients are added at the edge of the bowl and only stirred in after the yeast has been mixed with the flour. Yeast processes sugar quickly, but it needs to break down the flour before it can digest it.

Once the yeasty liquid has been incorporated into the flour, proceed as for the other type of dried yeast. Use the dough hook of a hand mixer to knead the mixture, first at low speed and then at full speed, until it forms a smooth dough.
Only then add raisins, nuts, or other ingredients specified in the recipe.

Keep the dough covered (with a tea towel or clingfilm) in a warm place until it has visibly increased in size. The amount of the increase will depend on the recipe.
Yeast dough should never be baked immediately after preparation - it needs plenty time to rise. Leave it in a warm place, for example in a gas, electric or microwave oven (see below).

Shape the dough as instructed in the recipe. Once the dough is shaped, it will need to rest again so that it can rise again before baking. This second rising is called proving.
Baking sheets and baking tins generally need to be greased, preferably with spreadable margarine or butter, and sprinkled with cake or biscuit crumbs (depending on the recipe).

Leaving the dough to rise

Gas: Preheat the oven for three minutes at gas mark 8. **Turn off the gas**, and place the bowl of dough in the oven until it has visibly increased in size.
Electric: Set the oven to 50 °C/120°F. Place the bowl of dough in the oven until it has visibly increased in size. Wedge the oven door open with a wooden spoon.
Microwave: 80 or 90 watts, for about 8 minutes. If your microwave does not have a turntable, turn the bowl after about 4 minutes.
Bain-marie: Place the bowl of dough (covered with a damp cloth) in hot water until it has visibly increased in size.

Basic recipe
Grundrezept

500 g (1 lb 2 oz) strong plain flour
1 sachet dry yeast
75 g (2¾ oz) sugar
2 tsp vanilla sugar
1 pinch of salt
250 ml (9 fl oz) lukewarm milk
75–100 g (2 ½-3½ oz) melted and cooled margarine or butter or 6-7 tbsp vegetable oil

Sift the flour into a mixing bowl and carefully mix in the dry yeast. Add the sugar, vanilla sugar, salt, milk and melted margarine or butter or oil.

Alternative method for small baking sheets about 38 x 28 cm (15 x 11 inch):

375 g (13 oz) strong plain flour
1 sachet Easyblend dry yeast
50 g (2 oz) sugar
2 tsp vanilla sugar
1 pinch of salt
1 egg
200 ml (7 fl oz) lukewarm milk
50 g (2 oz) melted and cooled margarine or butter or 4-5 tbsp vegetable oil

Sift the flour into a mixing bowl and carefully mix in the dry yeast. Add the sugar, vanilla sugar, salt, egg, milk and melted margarine or butter or the oil.
Use the dough hook of a hand mixer to work the mixture into a dough, first at low speed and then at full speed, for about 5 minutes.
Cover the dough and keep it in a warm place until it has visibly increased in size (about 20 minutes). Dust it lightly with flour, remove it from the bowl and briefly knead it again on the work surface.
Depending on the recipe, leave the dough to rise again in a baking tin or on a baking sheet.
Bake according to the recipe instructions.

Baking yeast dough

Yeast dough should always be put in a warm place before baking, to allow it to rise once again.

Cover the dough with a tea towel to make it rise quickly.
Then process and bake the dough as specified in the recipe.

Triple-plaited Yeast Loaf

sophisticated

Hefezopf „Dreierlei" (see photo on pages 92/93)

For the dough

- 500 g (1 lb 2oz) strong plain flour
- 1 sachet Easyblend dry yeast
- 50 g (2 oz) sugar
- 2 tsp vanilla sugar
- 1 pinch salt
- 150 ml (5 fl oz) crème fraîche
- 150 ml (5 fl oz) lukewarm milk
- 75 g (2¾ oz) melted and cooled margarine or butter

Sift the flour into a mixing bowl and carefully mix in the dry yeast. Add the sugar, vanilla sugar, salt, crème fraîche, milk and melted margarine or butter.

Use the dough hook of a hand mixer to work the mixture into a dough, first at low speed, then at full speed for about 5 minutes. Keep the dough covered in a warm place until it has visibly increased in size.

For the filling

- 100 g (3½ oz) raisins
- 2 tbsp rum
- 4 canned pineapple rings
- 50 g (2 oz) desiccated coconut
- 70 g (2½ oz) unblanched almonds
- 100 g (3½ oz) marzipan

Mix the raisins with the rum and leave to stand for about 30 minutes. Thoroughly drain the pineapple rings, chop them finely and mix with the desiccated coconut. Chop the almonds coarsely, cut the marzipan into cubes and combine the two ingredients.

- 1 egg yolk
- 1 tbsp milk

Lightly dust the risen dough with flour, remove it from the bowl and briefly knead it again on the work surface. Divide the dough into six equal portions. Knead the pineapple mixture into two portions, the soaked raisins into two portions and the almond mixture into the remaining two portions. Shape each portion into a roll about 30 cm (12 inch) in length and form two plaits. Place the plaits on a greased baking sheet and leave them to rise in a warm place until they have visibly increased in size.

Beat the egg yolk with the milk and brush over the plaits.

Oven temperatures

Conventional oven	170–200°C/350–400°F (preheated)
Fan-assisted oven	160–170°C/325°F (not preheated)
Gas oven	mark 3–4 (preheated)
Baking time	about 35 minutes.

Tip When kneading in the fillings, it may be necessary to add a little more flour.

Variations

Filling A

200 g (7 oz) marzipan
2 eggs
2 tbsp apricot jam
2 tbsp apricot liqueur or orange juice
200 g (7 oz) dried apricots
50 g (2 oz) finely chopped banana chips

Beat the marzipan with the eggs, jam and apricot liqueur or orange juice until smooth. Cut the dried apricots into cubes and fold into the marzipan mixture with the chopped banana chips.

Filling B

175 g (6 oz) ground poppyseeds
125 ml (4 fl oz) double cream
2 large apples (400 g/14 oz)

Alternatively, mix the ground poppy seeds with the double cream. Grate the apples coarsely and fold into the mixture. Roll out the dough to form two 30 x 40 cm (12 x 15 inch) rectangles and cut into three strips, starting from the longest side. Place the filling on top and roll up each strip like a Swiss roll, then plait the strips.

Saxon Bilberry Cake

Sächsicher Heidelbeerkuchen

traditional

For the dough

375 g (13 oz) strong plain flour
1 sachet Easyblend dry yeast
50 g (2 oz) sugar
2 tsp vanilla sugar
1 pinch salt
1 egg
2 egg yolks
200 ml (7 fl oz) lukewarm milk
50 g (2 oz) melted and cooled margarine or butter

Sift the flour into a mixing bowl and carefully mix in the dry yeast. Add the sugar, vanilla sugar, salt, egg, egg yolks, milk and the melted margarine or butter.
Use the dough hook of a hand mixer to work the mixture into a dough, first at low speed and then at full speed for about 5 minutes.
Cover the dough and keep it in a warm place until it has visibly increased in size. Lightly dust it with flour, remove it from the bowl and briefly knead it again on the work surface. Roll out the dough on a greased 38 x 28 cm (15 x 11 inch) baking sheet or Swiss roll tin. Place a folded strip of aluminium foil in front of the dough if one side of the baking sheet is flat.
Leave the dough to rise for a further 15 minutes.

(continued on page 100)

For the topping

1 kg (2 lb 4 oz) bilberries or blueberries 50 g (2 oz) butter 5 tbsp cake or biscuit crumbs 100 g (3½ oz) sugar 1 tsp ground cinnamon 50 g (1¾ oz) butter, cut into small pieces	Wash the bilberries or blueberries and drain thoroughly. Melt the butter and brush over the dough. Sprinkle 3 tablespoons of the cake or biscuit crumbs over the dough and spread the bilberries or blueberries evenly on top. Mix the sugar with the cinnamon and sprinkle over the bilberries or blueberries. Dot with the butter and sprinkle with the remaining crumbs.

Oven temperatures	
Conventional oven	about 220°C/425°F (preheated)
Fan-assisted oven	about 200°C/400°F (not preheated)
Gas oven	mark 4-5 (preheated)
Baking time	about 25 minutes.

Apple or Crumble or Plum Cake

traditional

Apfel-, Streusel- oder Pflaumenkuchen

For the dough

375 g (13 oz) strong plain flour 1 sachet Easyblend dry yeast 50 g (2 oz) sugar 2 tsp vanilla sugar 1 pinch salt 1 egg 200 ml (7 fl oz) lukewarm milk 50 g (2 oz) melted and cooled margarine or butter	Sift the flour into a mixing bowl and carefully mix in the dry yeast. Add the sugar, vanilla sugar, salt, egg, milk and the melted margarine or butter. Use the dough hook of a hand mixer to work the mixture into a dough, first at low speed and then at full speed for about 5 minutes. Cover the dough and keep it in a warm place until it has visibly increased in size. Lightly dust it with flour, remove it from the bowl and briefly knead it again on the work surface. Roll out the dough to fit a greased 38 x 28 cm (15 x 11 inch) baking sheet or Swiss roll tin. Place a folded strip of aluminium foil in front of the dough if one side of the baking sheet is flat.

For the apple cake

about 1 ½ kg (3 lb 5 oz) apples 20 g (¾ oz) blanched, slivered almonds 20 g (¾ oz) raisins	Peel, quarter, core and thickly slice the apples. Spread them evenly over the dough and scatter the almonds and raisins on top. Leave the dough to rise again in a warm place until it has visibly increased in size.

(continued on page 102)

Oven temperatures	
Conventional oven	200–220°C/400–425°F (preheated)
Fan-assisted oven	about 180°C/350°F (not preheated)
Gas oven	mark 3–4 (preheated)
Baking time	20–30 minutes.

For the apricot glaze

3 tbsp apricot jam
1 tbsp water

Mix the apricot jam and water in a pan and bring to the boil, stirring continuously. Brush over the apple cake immediately after baking.

For the crumble topping

300 g (10½ oz) plain flour
150 g (5½ oz) sugar
2 tsp vanilla sugar
150-200 g (5½-7 oz) margarine or butter

Sift the flour into a mixing bowl and mix in the sugar and vanilla sugar. Add the margarine or butter and use the dough hook of a hand mixer to process the ingredients until they have the consistency of coarse breadcrumbs. Sprinkle the topping evenly over the dough.
Leave the dough to rise again in a warm place until it has visibly increased in size.

Oven temperatures	
Conventional oven	200–220°C/400–425°F (preheated)
Fan-assisted oven	170–180°C/350°F (not preheated)
Gas oven	mark 3–4 (preheated)
Baking time	15–20 minutes.

For the plum cake

2 ½ kg (5 lb 8 oz) ripe plums

Wash the plums and drain thoroughly. Wipe each plum with a cloth, remove the stones and arrange them on the dough with the cut sides upwards, so that they overlap.
Leave the dough to rise again in a warm place until it has visibly increased in size.

Oven temperatures	
Conventional oven	200–220°C/400–425°F (preheated)
Fan-assisted oven	170–180°C/350°F (not preheated)
Gas oven	mark 3–4 (preheated)
Baking time	20–30 minutes.

Granulated sugar

Allow the cake to cool slightly, then sprinkle with sugar.

Marzipan Crunch Cake

Marzipan-Krokant-Kuchen

popular

375 g (13 oz) strong plain flour
1 sachet Easyblend dry yeast
75 g ($2^{3}/_{4}$ oz) sugar
2 tsp vanilla sugar
1 egg
200 ml (7 fl oz) lukewarm double cream
50 g (2 oz) melted and cooled margarine or butter

For the dough

Sift the flour into a mixing bowl and carefully mix in the dry yeast. Add the sugar, vanilla sugar, egg, cream and melted margarine or butter.

Use the dough hook of a hand mixer to work the mixture into a dough, first at low speed and then at full speed for about 5 minutes. Cover the dough and keep it in a warm place until it has visibly increased in size.

200 g (7 oz) marzipan
2 eggs
2 tbsp apricot jam
2 tbsp apricot liqueur
200 g (7 oz) dried apricots, finely chopped
100 g ($3^{1}/_{2}$ oz) blanched, slivered almonds

For the filling

Beat the marzipan, eggs, apricot jam and liqueur with an electric whisk until smooth. Stir in the chopped dried apricots and slivered almonds.

Lightly dust the risen dough with flour, remove it from the bowl and briefly knead it again on the work surface. Roll out half the dough on a greased 38 x 23 cm (15 x 9 inch) baking sheet and spread the filling evenly on top.

Roll out the other half of the dough to form a 38 x 23 cm (15 x 9 inch) rectangle. Cover with non-stick baking paper and roll it up then unroll it over the filling. Prick several times with a fork. Place a pleated strip of aluminium foil in front of the dough if one side of the baking sheet is open.

Leave the dough to rise again in a warm place until it has visibly increased in size.

30 g ($1^{1}/_{4}$ oz) butter
30 g ($1^{1}/_{4}$ oz) sugar
2 tsp vanilla sugar
40 g ($1^{1}/_{2}$ oz) honey
3 tbsp double cream
50 g (2 oz) blanched, ground almonds
100 g ($3^{1}/_{2}$ oz) blanched, slivered almonds

For the topping

Heat the butter, sugar, vanilla sugar, honey, cream and ground almonds in a pan. Allow to boil for one minute while stirring and add the slivered almonds.

Spread the mixture carefully over the risen dough.

(continued on page 104)

Oven temperatures	
Conventional oven	170–200°C/350–400°F (preheated)
Fan-assisted oven	150–180°C/300–350°F (not preheated)
Gas oven	mark 3–4 (preheated)
Baking time	about 20 minutes.

Thuringian Coconut Cake

Kokoskuchen aus Thüringen

easy

For the dough

- 375 g (13 oz) strong plain flour
- 1 sachet Easyblend dry yeast
- 50 g (2 oz) sugar
- 2 tsp vanilla sugar
- 1 egg
- 200 ml (7 fl oz) lukewarm milk
- 50 g (2 oz) melted and cooled margarine or butter

Sift the flour into a mixing bowl and carefully mix in the dry yeast. Add the sugar, vanilla sugar, egg, milk and melted margarine or butter.

Use the dough hook of a hand mixer to work the mixture into a dough, first at low speed and then at full speed for about 5 minutes. Cover the dough and keep it in a warm place until it has visibly increased in size.

For the topping

- 200 g (7 oz) butter
- 150 g (5½ oz) sugar
- 2 tsp vanilla sugar
- 200 g (7 oz) desiccated coconut
- 3 eggs
- 20 g (¾ oz) softened butter

Melt the butter and add the sugar and vanilla sugar. Bring to the boil, stirring continuously. Stir in the desiccated coconut and allow to brown slightly. Leave the mixture to cool and beat in the eggs.

Lightly dust the risen dough with flour, remove it from the bowl and briefly knead it again on the work surface. Roll out the dough on a greased 38 x 28 cm (15 x 11 inch) baking sheet or Swiss roll tin and brush with the melted butter. Place a folded strip of aluminium foil in front of the dough if one side of the baking sheet is open. Spread the topping over the dough and bake immediately.

Oven temperatures	
Conventional oven	200–220°C/400–425°F (not preheated, bottom shelf)
Fan-assisted oven	170–180°C/350°F (not preheated)
Gas oven	mark 4–5 (not preheated)
Baking time	about 25 minutes.

150 ml (5 fl oz) hot milk — Brush the milk over the cake while it is still hot and leave to cool.

Tip Drizzle 50 g (2 oz) melted chocolate over the cake when it has cooled.

Beestings
Bienenstich

traditional

For the dough

- 375 g (13 oz) strong plain flour
- 1 sachet Easyblend dry yeast
- 50 g (2 oz) sugar
- 2 tsp vanilla sugar
- 1 pinch salt
- 1 egg
- 200 ml (7 fl oz) lukewarm milk
- 50 g (2 oz) melted and cooled margarine or butter

Sift the flour into a mixing bowl and carefully mix in the dry yeast. Add the sugar, vanilla sugar, salt, egg, milk and melted margarine or butter.

Use the dough hook of a hand mixer to work the mixture into a dough, first at low speed and then at full speed for about 5 minutes. Cover the dough and keep it in a warm place until it has visibly increased in size.

For the topping

- 150 g (5½ oz) butter
- 75 g (2¾ oz) sugar
- 2 tsp vanilla sugar
- 1 tbsp honey
- 3 tbsp double cream
- 150 g (5½ oz) blanched, slivered almonds

Gently heat the butter, sugar, vanilla sugar, honey and cream in a pan, stirring continuously. Allow to boil for a short time. Add the slivered almonds and leave to cool, stirring occasionally.

Lightly dust the risen dough with flour, remove it from the bowl and briefly knead it again on the work surface. Roll out the dough in a greased 38 x 28 cm (15 x 11 inch) Swiss roll tin. Spread the topping evenly over the dough (photo 1) and leave it to rise until it has visibly increased in size.

(continued on page 108)

Oven temperatures	
Conventional oven	200–220°C/400–425°F (preheated)
Fan-assisted oven	180–200°C/350–400°F (not preheated)
Gas oven	mark 3–4 (preheated)
Baking time	12–15 minutes.

For the filling

2 packets vanilla pudding powder
750 ml (1¼ pints) milk
100 g (3½ oz) sugar
100 g (3½ oz) butter

Make the vanilla pudding according to the instructions on the packet, adding the sugar but not using more than 750 ml (1¼ pints) milk. Immediately stir in the butter and leave to cool, stirring occasionally.
When the cake has cooled, cut it in half. Cut each half into two layers (photo 2) and spread with the filling (photo 3).

Vanilla Slices

for guests

Gefüllte Schnitten

For the yeast dough

200 g (7 oz) strong plain flour
1 sachet Easyblend dry yeast
25 g (1 oz) sugar
2 tsp vanilla sugar
1 egg yolk
150 ml (5 fl oz) crème fraîche

Sift the flour into a mixing bowl and carefully mix in the dry yeast. Add the sugar, vanilla sugar, egg yolk and crème fraîche.
Use the dough hook of a hand mixer to work the mixture into a dough, first at low speed and then at full speed for about 5 minutes. Cover the dough and keep it in a warm place until it has visibly increased in size.

For the strudel dough

300 g (10½ oz) (5 sheets) strudel or phyllo dough

Grease a Swiss roll tin and rinse it with water. Cover the sheets of strudel or phyllo dough with a damp cloth and defrost at room temperature. Arrange the sheets so that the edges overlap slightly. Trim the sheets to the dimensions of the Swiss roll tin and place in the tin. Prick several times with a fork and leave to stand for about 30 minutes.

Oven temperatures	
Conventional oven	about 220 °C/425°F (preheated)
Fan-assisted oven	180–200°C/350–400°F (not preheated)
Gas oven	mark 3–4 (preheated)
Baking time	about 20 minutes.

Leave the strudel dough to cool slightly.

For the filling

2 packets vanilla pudding powder 700 ml (1¼ pints) milk 80 g (2¾ oz) sugar 250 ml (9 fl oz) crème fraîche	Make the vanilla pudding according to the instructions on the packet, using the ingredients specified here. Allow to cool slightly and stir in the crème fraîche. Spread the filling over the strudel dough.

Dust the risen yeast dough lightly with flour, remove it from the bowl and briefly knead it again on the work surface. Roll out to the dimensions of the Swiss roll tin and place on top of the filling.

For the topping

100 g (3½ oz) margarine or butter 100 g (3½ oz) sugar 2 tbsp milk or single cream 100 g (3½ oz) blanched, slivered almonds	Bring the margarine or butter, sugar and milk or cream to the boil, stirring continuously. Add the slivered almonds and allow to cool slightly. Spread the topping evenly over the yeast dough. Leave the dough to rise again in a warm place until it has visibly increased in size.

Oven temperatures

Conventional oven	about 180 °C/350°F (preheated)
Fan-assisted oven	about 150 °C/300°F (not preheated)
Gas oven	mark 3–4 (preheated)
Baking time	about 30 minutes.

Tip

200 g (7 oz) plain flour 70 g (2½ oz) blanched, ground almonds 150 g (5½ oz) sugar 150-200 g (5½-7 oz) margarine or butter	Alternatively, you could use a crumble topping. For this, sift the flour into a bowl and add the ground almonds, sugar and margarine or butter. Use the dough hook of a hand mixer and knead until the mixture resembles coarse breadcrumbs. Sprinkle the crumble evenly over the yeast dough.

Thuringian Crumble Cake

Streuselkuchen aus Thüringen

sophisticated

For the dough

375 g (13 oz) strong plain flour
1 sachet Easyblend dry yeast
50 g (2 oz) sugar
2 tsp vanilla sugar
1 pinch salt
1 egg
200 ml (7 fl oz) lukewarm milk
50 g (2 oz) melted and cooled margarine or butter

Sift the flour into a mixing bowl and carefully mix in the dry yeast. Add the sugar, vanilla sugar, salt, egg, milk and melted margarine or butter.
Use the dough hook of a hand mixer to work the mixture into a dough, first at low speed and then at full speed for about 5 minutes.
Cover the dough and keep it in a warm place until it has visibly increased in size. Dust it lightly with flour, remove it from the bowl and briefly knead it again on the work surface.

20 g (¾ oz) melted butter

Roll out the dough on a greased 38 x 28 cm (15 x 11 inch) baking sheet and brush with the melted butter. Place a folded strip of aluminium foil in front of the dough if one side of the baking sheet is open.

For the crumble topping

300 g (10½ oz) plain flour
150 g (5½ oz) sugar
2 tsp vanilla sugar
200 g (7 oz) softened butter or margarine

Sift the flour into a bowl and mix in the sugar and vanilla sugar. Add the softened butter or margarine. Use the dough hook of a hand mixer and knead until the mixture resembles coarse breadcrumbs (photo 1). Sprinkle the crumble evenly over the yeast dough.

(continued on page 112)

2 tsp cocoa powder	Mix the cocoa powder into the remaining mixture and fill in the gaps on the dough, creating a chequered pattern (photo 2). Leave the dough to rise again in a warm place until it has visibly increased in size.
Oven temperatures	
Conventional oven	200–220°C/400–425°F (preheated)
Fan-assisted oven	180–200°C/350–400°F (not preheated)
Gas oven	mark 4–5 (preheated)
Baking time	15–20 minutes.

The finishing touch

125 ml (4 fl oz) milk
160 g (6½ oz) butter
50 g (2 oz) icing sugar

Heat the milk and 60 g (2½ oz) of the butter in a pan until the butter has dissolved. Drizzle over the cake while it is still warm. Leave the cake to cool, melt the rest of the butter and pour it over the cake (photo 3). Dust with icing sugar.

Butter Cake

Butterkuchen

easy

For the dough

375 g (13 oz) strong plain flour
1 sachet Easyblend dry yeast
50 g (2 oz) sugar
2 tsp vanilla sugar
1 pinch salt
1 egg
200 ml (7 fl oz) lukewarm milk
50 g (2 oz) melted, cooled butter

Sift the flour into a mixing bowl and carefully mix in the dry yeast. Add the sugar, vanilla sugar, salt, egg, milk and melted butter.
Use the dough hook of a hand mixer to work the mixture into a dough, first at low speed and then at full speed for about 5 minutes.
Cover the dough and keep it in a warm place until it has visibly increased in size. Dust it lightly with flour, remove it from the bowl and briefly knead it again on the work surface.
Roll out the dough on a greased 38 x 28 cm (15 x 11 inch) baking sheet and brush with the melted butter. Place a folded strip of aluminium foil in front of the dough if one side of the baking sheet is open.

For the topping

100 g (3½ oz) butter
75 g (2¾ oz) sugar
2 tsp vanilla sugar
100 g (3½ oz) blanched, slivered almonds

Cut the butter into pieces. Make shallow depressions in the dough (photo 1) and dot the butter evenly over the dough. Alternatively, melt the butter and brush it over the dough. Mix the sugar with the vanilla sugar and sprinkle over the top (photo 2). Sprinkle the slivered almonds evenly over the top (photo 3). Leave the dough to rise again in a warm place until it has visibly increased in size.

Oven temperatures

Conventional oven	200–220°C/400–425°F (preheated)
Fan-assisted oven	180–200°C/350–400°F (not preheated)
Gas oven	mark 3–4 (preheated)
Baking time	about 15 minutes.

Leave the cake to cool on the baking sheet and then slice into bars.

Tip Whip 250 ml (9 fl oz) cream until stiff and spread evenly over the butter cake immediately after baking.

Variation

Butter Cake with a Nut Crust

100 g (3½ oz) hazelnuts or walnuts
100 g (3½ oz) butter, cut into pieces
sugar mixed with ground cinnamon
8 tbsp double cream

Coarsely chop the hazelnuts or walnuts and sprinkle them over the yeast dough. Dot the dough evenly with the pieces of butter and sprinkle with the sugar mixture. Drizzle about 8 tablespoons of cream over the dough and leave it to rise in a warm place until it has visibly increased in size. Bake as above.

Gugelhupf

Feiner Gugelhupf

traditional

1 sachet dry yeast or 2 tbsp fresh yeast 1 tsp sugar 200 ml (7 fl oz) lukewarm double cream 500 g (1 lb 2oz) strong plain flour 150 g (5½ oz) sugar 2 tsp vanilla sugar 6 drops of lemon essence 1 pinch salt 4 eggs	Carefully mix together the yeast, sugar and lukewarm cream in a bowl and leave to stand at room temperature for 15 minutes. Sift the flour into a mixing bowl and make a well in the centre. Place the sugar, vanilla sugar, lemon essence, salt, eggs and melted, cooled butter around the edge of the flour. Pour the yeast mixture into the well in the centre.
200 g (7 oz) melted, cooled butter	Use the dough hook of a hand mixer to work the mixture into a dough, first at low speed and then at full speed for about 5 minutes.
150 g (5½ oz) raisins 150 g (5½ oz) currants 100 g (3¼ oz) unblanched, coarsely chopped almonds	Add the raisins, currants and chopped almonds to the dough. Cover the dough and keep it in a warm place until it has visibly increased in size, then briefly knead it again at full speed. Place the dough in a greased gugelhupf mould and leave to rise again in a warm place until it has visibly increased in size.
Oven temperatures	
Conventional oven	170–200°C/375–400°F (preheated)
Fan-assisted oven	160–170°C/325–350°F (not preheated)
Gas oven	mark 2–3 (not preheated)
Baking time	about 1 hour.
4 tsp icing sugar	Leave the gugelhupf in the mould for about 10 minutes after baking, then turn out and leave to cool. Dust with icing sugar.

Apple Turnovers
Apfeltaschen

for children

For the filling

- 500 g (1 lb 2oz) apples
- 50 g (2 oz) raisins
- 40 g (1½ oz) sugar
- 20 g (¾ oz) butter

Peel, quarter, core and finely chop the apples. Place in a pan and gently stew with the raisins, sugar and butter, stirring continuously. Leave to cool.

For the dough

- 375 g (13 oz) strong plain flour
- 1 sachet Easyblend dry yeast
- 50 g (2 oz)sugar
- 2 tsp vanilla sugar
- 1 pinch salt
- 1 egg
- 200 ml (7 fl oz) lukewarm milk
- 50 g (2 oz) melted and cooled margarine or butter

Sift the flour into a mixing bowl and carefully mix in the dry yeast. Add the sugar, vanilla sugar, salt, egg, milk and melted margarine or butter.

Use the dough hook of a hand mixer to work the mixture into a dough, first at low speed and then at full speed for about 5 minutes.

Cover the dough and keep it in a warm place until it has visibly increased in size. Dust it lightly with flour, remove it from the bowl and briefly knead it again on the work surface. Roll it out thinly and use a biscuit cutter to cut out circles about 12 cm (4½ inches) in diameter (photo 1).

Put some of the apple mixture on half of each circle (photo 2) and brush the edges of the dough with milk. Fold the other half of the dough over the filling. Press the edges together firmly (photo 3).

(continued on page 118)

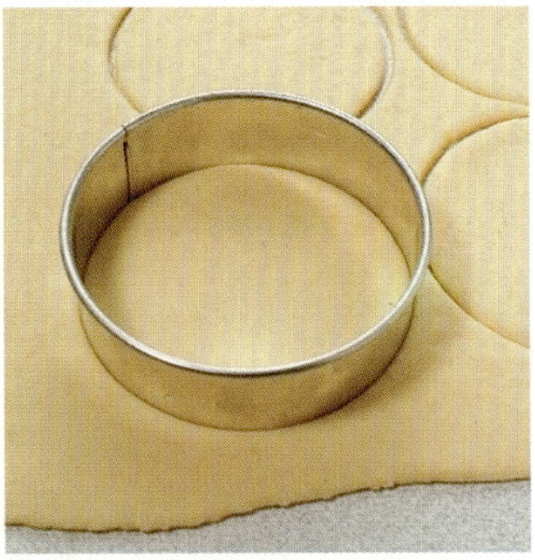

milk	Brush the turnovers with milk and sprinkle the slivered almonds on top. Place the turnovers on a baking sheet lined with non-stick baking paper and leave them to rise in a warm place until they have visibly increased in size.
blanched, slivered almonds	
Oven temperatures	
Conventional oven	200–220°C/400–425°F (preheated)
Fan-assisted oven	170–180°C/350°F (not preheated)
Gas oven	mark 3–4 (preheated)
Baking time	about 15 minutes.

For the glaze

100 g (3½ oz) icing sugar	Sift the icing sugar and mix with the lemon juice until smooth. Stir in the melted butter. Brush over the turnovers immediately after baking.
1 tbsp lemon juice	
10 g (¼ oz) melted butter	

Tip Use sour cherries, peaches or apricots instead of apples. If desired, the fruit can be sprinkled with 50-100 g (2-3½ oz) slivered almonds.

Cake with Quark and Raisin Topping

traditional

Eierschecke

For the dough

300 g (10½ oz) strong plain flour
1 sachet Easyblend dry yeast
50 g (2 oz) sugar
2 tsp vanilla sugar
4 drops lemon essence
1 pinch salt
1 egg
125 ml (4 fl oz) lukewarm milk
100 g (3½ oz) melted and cooled margarine or butter

Sift the flour into a mixing bowl and carefully mix in the dry yeast. Add the sugar, vanilla sugar, lemon essence, salt, egg, milk and melted margarine or butter.

Use the dough hook of a hand mixer to work the mixture into a dough, first at low speed and then at full speed for about 5 minutes. Cover the dough and keep it in a warm place until it has visibly increased in size.

For the cheese topping

1 packet vanilla pudding powder
40 g (1½ oz) sugar
500 ml (18 fl oz) milk
500 g (1 lb 2oz) low-fat soft cheese
65 g (2½ oz) raisins

Make the vanilla pudding according to the instructions on the packet, using the ingredients specified here. Place in a bowl, cover with clingfilm and leave to cool. Stir in the low-fat soft cheese and the raisins.

Dust the risen dough lightly with flour, remove it from the bowl and briefly knead it again on the work surface. Roll out in a greased Swiss roll tin and spread the cheese mixture on top.

For the egg creme

125 g (4½ oz) softened butter
125 g (4½ oz) sugar
4 egg yolks
4 egg whites
15 g (½ oz) cornflour

Using the whisk of a hand mixer, beat the softened butter until smooth and gradually add the sugar. Keep whisking until the mixture binds together. Gradually beat in the egg yolks. Whisk the egg whites until stiff and add to the mixture. Sift the cornflour over the top and gently fold in.
Spread the creme over the cheese topping, smooth the surface and bake immediately.

Oven temperatures

Conventional oven	170–200°C/350–400°F (preheated)
Fan-assisted oven	150–180 °C/300–350°F (not preheated)
Gas oven	mark 3–4 (preheated)
Baking time	about 30 minutes.

Tip Soak the raisins in 2 tablespoons of rum before use.

Vanilla Pinwheels

Puddingschnecken

suitable for freezing

For the dough

- 500 g (1 lb 2oz) strong plain flour
- 1 sachet Easyblend dry yeast
- 50 g (2 oz) sugar
- 2 tsp vanilla sugar
- 1 pinch salt
- 2 eggs
- 125 ml (4 fl oz) lukewarm milk
- 100 g (3½ oz) melted, cooled margarine or butter

Sift the flour into a mixing bowl and carefully mix in the dry yeast. Add the sugar, vanilla sugar, salt, eggs, milk and melted margarine or butter.
Use the dough hook of a hand mixer to work the mixture into a dough, first at low speed and then at full speed for about 5 minutes.
Cover the dough and keep it in a warm place until it has visibly increased in size.

For the filling

- 2 packets vanilla pudding powder
- 750 ml (1¼ pints) milk
- 80 g (2¾ oz) sugar
- 100 g (3½ oz) raisins

Make the vanilla pudding according to the instructions on the packet, adding the sugar but not using more than 750 ml (1¼ pints) milk. Leave to cool, stirring occasionally. Add the raisins.

Dust the risen dough lightly with flour, remove it from the bowl and briefly knead it again on the work surface. Roll out to form a 40 x 60 cm (16 x 24 inch) rectangle and spread the filling on top. Roll up the dough, starting from the shortest end, and cut into 2 cm (1 inch) slices. Place on greased baking sheets lined with non-stick baking paper.
Leave the dough to rise again in a warm place until it has visibly increased in size.

Oven temperatures

Conventional oven	200–220°C/400–425°F (preheated)
Fan-assisted oven	180–200°C/350–400°F (not preheated)
Gas oven	mark 3–4 (preheated)
Baking time	10–15 minutes.

For the apricot glaze

- 2 tbsp apricot jam
- 1 tbsp water

Press the apricot jam through a sieve, add the water and bring briefly to the boil, stirring continuously. Glaze the pinwheels immediately after baking.

Preparation

When baking sponge cakes, the base of the baking sheets and tins must be lined with non-stick baking paper (Fig. a-c).

We recommend lining the base of springform tins, cake tins and baking sheets with non-stick baking paper.

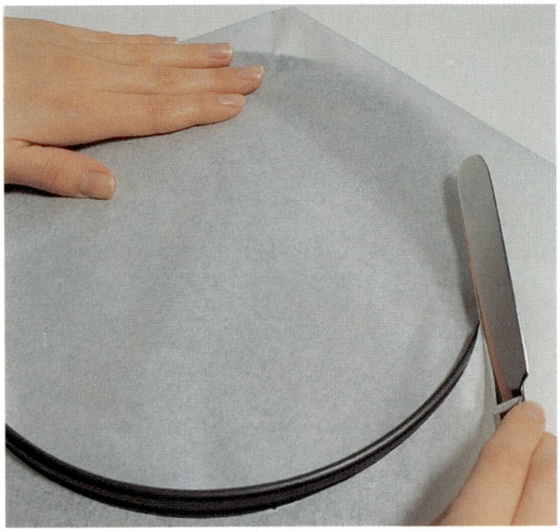

a) For a springform tin, cut the paper as follows: turn the tin over (base upwards) and place the paper on top. Use the back of a knife to trim the excess paper from around the edge.

b) Greasing the tin.
Grease the base at about 4 points with spreadable margarine or butter, preferably using a pastry brush. **Do not grease the ring or sides.**

c) Press the paper on to the base. To do this, lay the paper on the base of the assembled springform tin, starting at one side. Smooth it out with your hands to make sure there are no uneven areas or folds.

The individual steps

Eggs
Fresh eggs should always be used for baking. Nonetheless, each egg should be broken into a cup to check for freshness. Eggs are added towards the end of the recipe, and a bad egg will spoil all the other ingredients.

Use the whisk of a hand mixer to whisk the eggs and hot water for 1 minute at full speed, until foamy.
Add the water to the eggs. If varying quantities of water are specified in the recipe, this is because the amount of water depends on the size of the eggs. Use more water for small eggs, less water for large eggs.

Whisk in the sugar (mixed with the vanilla sugar, if used) or honey for 1 minute. Then whisk for about 2 more minutes. Add spices and flavourings to the egg mixture.

Mix the flour with baking powder and cornflour and sift half of it over the liquids. Briefly whisk in at low speed. Work in the rest of the flour in the same way.
Mixing and sifting breaks up the flour and distributes the other dry ingredients evenly throughout the mixture. This makes the cake much lighter.
If using **wholemeal** flour, mix the baking powder with the flour and whisk it into the mixture in two portions, at low speed.
If using almonds or other nuts, make sure that they are coarsely ground. Nuts are very high in fat; if they are too finely ground, they will make the sponge tough and hard.

Place the mixture in the lined tin or sheet.
It is best to use a dough scraper to transfer the mixture into the prepared tin and spread it out evenly.

Baking sponge mixtures

Sponge mixtures must always be baked immediately after preparation, following the instructions in the recipe.
Check that the sponge is cooked before removing it from the oven. The best method is to briefly hold the flat of the hand against the surface. If the sponge is ready, it will no longer feel moist and the texture should feel soft, almost like cotton wool. If it has been baked for too long, it will be dry and hard. **Fan-assisted ovens are not suitable for baking sponge mixtures**, which is why no fan oven temperatures are given in this chapter.

When the sponge has cooled slightly, run a knife around the edge to release it from the springform tin and remove the side of the tin.

Place the sponge on a wire rack to cool properly. If it is not going to be iced or eaten until the next day, leave the paper on until then.

Filling a sponge cake

Place the sponge on a sheet of paper in such a way that the bottom, which is particularly smooth, faces upwards.
It can be cut into layers using a piece of thread or a large knife. To ensure that the layers are of equal thickness, first run a small, sharp knife around the edge of the sponge to a depth of about 1 cm (½ inch).

Place the thread in the incision, cross over the ends and pull firmly together, thus cutting through the cake.

To make sure that the layer does not break, slide it off using a sheet of paper. To do so, fold the front edge of the paper underneath and slide it under the upper layer. From time to time, use your index fingers to keep the upper layer in place, so that the paper is pulled through the middle.

Lift off the upper layer.
Try to keep the paper as flat as possible, as the cake could easily break.

If you are cutting through the sponge with a knife, it is best to use a knife which is longer than the width of the cake.

Various kinds of jam or marmalade are suitable for filling the cake, as is buttercream made with pudding or custard powder. If using buttercream, another option is to spread one layer with buttercream and another with jam, using a knife, dough scraper or palette knife.

Use the paper to arrange the two layers back on top of one another. It is important for the edges of the layers to be aligned.

Spread buttercream over the other layer and place the third layer on top.

Spread a thin layer of buttercream over the top and sides of the cake, followed by the rest of the buttercream. It is best to use a table knife to spread it around the sides.

Decorating the filled cake

Sprinkle the sides of the cake with chocolate flakes, chopped almonds, ground hazelnuts or toasted oats. One method is to hold the flakes or nuts very close to the cake and to spread them up the sides with a dough scraper or a knife.

Before decorating the cake, use a cake divider to mark out the slices on the top.

Hold the piping bag upright when decorating the cake. Use your right hand to hold the bag and press out the cream or buttercream and use your left hand to guide the bag. Do not grasp the bag with your whole hand, but guide the nozzle or nozzle attachment with your thumb and index finger. Otherwise the warmth of your hand will make the cream or buttercream too loose. This buttercream cake is decorated with swirls placed close together. For each marked portion, place the piping bag in the middle and work your way towards the edge.

For the marzipan mixture, knead 50 g (2 oz) icing sugar into 200 g (7 oz) marzipan. Roll out the finished mixture between sheets of cling-film.

Place the base of a springform tin on the rolled-out marzipan as a template for the top of the cake. Cut round it with a pastry cutter or a knife.

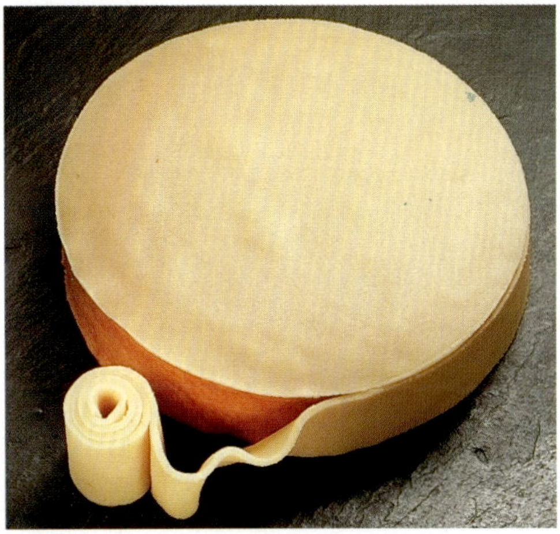

Roll out the marzipan for the sides. Measure the circumference and height of the cake. Cut out a strip of marzipan and roll it up. Hold the roll against the side of the cake, unroll it and press it gently into position.

Strawberry cake
Spread strawberry-flavoured cream evenly over the sides of the cake. Pile the rest of the cream on top of the cake. Smooth it out slightly, make small indentations with a teaspoon and decorate with strawberries and chopped pistachio nuts.

Exotic cake
Spread some of the cream or buttercream over the entire cake. Place the rest in a piping bag with a small, plain nozzle. Pipe equal-sized dots over the cake and decorate with exotic fruit, such as physalis (Cape gooseberries) half-dipped in chocolate.

Colourful cake
Place a strip of coloured marzipan around the sides of the cake (see page 162) and fray the top edge with a pair of scissors. Purée canned, fresh or frozen fruit (or press jam through a sieve) and spread it over the top of the cake. Trace patterns with the handle of a cooking spoon to create a marbled effect.
Decorate with pieces of marzipan if liked.

Icing the cake

Before applying icing, brush the cake with apricot jam so that the icing does not sink in. Use a smooth jam or jelly for this purpose - lumpy jam should first be pressed through a sieve and then brought to the boil, stirring continuously, possibly with a little water.
Pour the icing on to the middle of the cake.

Tilt the cake to distribute the icing evenly over the top and sides.

It is important for the cake to be transferred to a cake dish as quickly as possible (using a large knife). First, use the knife to release the cake from the dish. By holding the dish at a slight angle and guiding the cake with the knife, you will be able to slide it carefully on to the cake dish.

Step-by-step instructions for making a Swiss roll

Line the baking sheet or Swiss roll tin with non-stick baking paper .
To do this, grease the sheet or tin at about 3 points with spreadable margarine or butter, preferably using a brush. Lay the paper on top and press down firmly. If using a baking sheet, make a fold at the open side of the tray to form an edge (so that the mixture cannot escape). Spread the mixture in the prepared tin.

When the sponge comes out of the oven, immediately run a knife around the edges to free it from the baking sheet and the paper. Use the paper to lift up the sponge and turn it on to a tea towel which has been sprinkled with sugar.

Brush the non-stick baking paper with cold water and remove it quickly but carefully from the sponge.

Immediately roll up the sponge using the tea towel and leave it to cool, or brush with jam. It is advisable to distribute the quantity of jam specified in the recipe evenly over the sponge with a tablespoon and then to quickly spread it out with a dough scraper.

Quickly roll up the sponge. This must be done without delay, as the cooler the sponge, the more likely it is to break when it is rolled up. The tea towel is used to help with the rolling process.

Classic Basic Recipe

Klassisches Grundrezept

For one sponge base for a Swiss roll or a Victoria Sponge

3-4 eggs	Use the whisk of a hand mixer to whisk the eggs and 3-4 tablespoons of hot water at full speed for 1 minute, until foamy.
3-4 tbsp hot water*	
150 g (5½ oz) sugar	Mix together the sugar and vanilla sugar and whisk in for 1 minute, then whisk for a further 2 minutes.
2 tsp vanilla sugar	
100 g (3½ oz) plain flour	Mix together the flour, cornflour and baking powder (use the smaller amount of baking powder if using 4 eggs). Sieve half onto the egg mixture and briefly whisk in at low speed. Work in the rest of the flour mixture in the same way.
100 g (3½ oz) cornflour	
2-3 tbsp baking powder (use less baking powder if 4 eggs are used)	
	Grease the base of a 28 cm (11 inch) springform tin and line it with non-stick baking paper. Bake the mixture according to the instructions.

For one Swiss roll

3 eggs 5-6 tbsp hot water* 150 g (5½ oz) sugar 2 tsp vanilla sugar 100 g (3½ oz) plain flour 50 g (2 oz) cornflour 1 tsp baking powder	Use the whisk of a hand mixer to whisk the eggs and 5-6 tablespoons of hot water at full speed for 1 minute, until foaming. Mix together the sugar and vanilla sugar and whisk in for 1 minute, then whisk for a further 2 minutes. Mix together the flour, cornflour and baking powder. Sift half on to the egg mixture and briefly whisk in at low speed. Work in the rest of the flour mixture in the same way. Spread the mixture in a greased baking sheet or Swiss roll tin lined with non-stick baking paper , to a depth of about 1 cm (½ inch). If using a baking sheet with an open side, fold the paper directly in front of the mixture to form an edge. Bake according to the instructions.

* Use less water for large eggs and more water for small eggs.

Basic Recipe: Dark-coloured Victoria sponge

Grundrezept dunkel, mit Fett

For one Victoria sponge cake

3 eggs 4 tbsp hot water 125 g (4½ oz) sugar 2 tsp vanilla sugar 75 g (2¾ oz) plain flour 65 g (2¼ oz) cornflour 15 g (½ oz) cocoa powder 2 tsp baking powder 75 g (2¾ oz) melted, cooled butter	Use the whisk of a hand mixer to whisk the eggs and 4 tablespoons of hot water at full speed for 1 minute, until foaming. Mix together the sugar and vanilla sugar and whisk in for 1 minute, then whisk for a further 2 minutes. Mix together the flour, cornflour, cocoa powder and baking powder. Sift half on to the egg mixture and briefly whisk in at low speed. Work in the rest of the flour mixture in the same way. Stir in the melted, slightly cooled butter. Line a 26-28 cm (11 inch) springform tin with non-stick baking paper and grease the base. Bake according to the instructions.

Strawberry Cream Cake

for special occasions

Erdbeer-Sahne-Torte (see photo on pages 122/123)

For the sponge mixture

- 2 eggs
- 2-3 tbsp hot water*
- 100 g (3½ oz) sugar
- 2 tsp vanilla sugar
- 75 g (2¾ oz) plain flour
- 50 g (2 oz) cornflour
- 1 tsp baking powder

Use the whisk of a hand mixer to whisk the eggs and 2-3 tablespoons of hot water at full speed for 1 minute, until foaming. Mix together the sugar and vanilla sugar and whisk in for 1 minute, then whisk for a further 2 minutes.

Mix together the flour, cornflour and baking powder. Sift half over the egg mixture and briefly whisk in at low speed. Work in the rest of the flour mixture in the same way.

Line a 26-28 cm (11 inch) springform tin with non-stick baking paper and grease the base. Bake according to the instructions.

Oven temperatures	
Conventional oven	170–200°C/375–400°F (preheated)
Fan-assisted oven	–
Gas oven	mark 3–4 (not preheated)
Baking time	20–30 minutes.

Loosen the sponge from the tin, turn out and leave to cool.

For the filling

- 1 packet custard powder
- 25 g (1 oz) sugar
- 250 ml (9 fl oz) milk

Make the custard according to the instructions on the packet, adding the sugar but not using more than 250 ml (9 fl oz) milk. Leave to cool, stirring occasionally.

- 500 g (1lb 2 oz) strawberries

Wash the strawberries and thoroughly drain them. Remove the stalks and cut the strawberries in half.

- 2 tsp unflavoured gelatine
- 3 tbsp cold water

Stir together the gelatine and water in small pan and leave to soak for 10 minutes. Heat until the gelatine has dissolved, stirring continuously.

- 500 ml (18 fl oz) double cream
- 40 g (1½ oz) icing sugar
- 2 tsp vanilla sugar

Whip the cream until almost stiff. Beat in the lukewarm gelatine solution and whip the cream until completely stiff. Sift the icing sugar, add the vanilla sugar and stir into the cream.

Cut the sponge into two layers and spread the filling over the bottom layer. Add the strawberries, spread three-quarters of the cream evenly over the top and press the upper layer firmly on top of the cream.

strawberries **blanched, slivered and toasted almonds**	Spread some of the remaining cream evenly over the top and sides. Decorate the cake with the rest of the cream, the strawberries and the slivered, toasted almonds.

* Use less water for large eggs and more for small eggs.

Malakoff Cake

for guests

Malakoff-Torte

150 g (5½ oz) butter **125 g (4½ oz) caster sugar** **2 tsp vanilla sugar** **3 egg yolks** **150 g (5½ oz) blanched, ground almonds** **125 ml (4 fl oz) double cream** **250 ml (9 fl oz) milk**	Use the hand mixer to cream the butter at full speed. Gradually whisk in the sugar and vanilla sugar until the mixture binds together. Gradually whisk in the egg yolks. Add the ground almonds and cream at medium speed.
2 tsp vanilla sugar **2-3 tbsp rum** **250 g (9 oz) sponge fingers**	Mix the milk with the vanilla sugar and rum, and briefly dip the sponge fingers into the mixture. Place the rim of a 26 cm (10½ inch) springform tin on a cake dish. Arrange half the sponge fingers on the bottom and spread half the cream mixture on top. Add the rest of the sponge fingers and the cream mixture and smooth the surface. Leave to cool (possibly overnight), then remove the rim of the springform tin.
250 ml (9 fl oz) whipping cream **1 tsp sugar** **2 tsp cream of tartar** **glacé or drained cocktail cherries**	Whip the cream for 30 seconds. Mix together the sugar and cream of tartar and sprinkle over the cream. Whip the cream until stiff. Put some of the cream in a piping bag with a star nozzle. Spread the rest of the cream over the top and sides of the cake. Decorate the cake with the cream in the piping bag and the cherries.

Black Forest Gateau
Schwarzwälder Kirschtorte

traditional / suitable for freezing

For the pastry base

125 g (4½ oz) plain flour
1 tbsp cocoa powder
1 pinch baking powder
50 g (1¾ oz) sugar
2 tsp vanilla sugar
1 tbsp kirsch
75 g (2¾ oz) margarine or butter

Mix the flour with the cocoa powder and baking powder and sieve into a mixing bowl. Add the sugar, vanilla sugar, kirsch and margarine or butter.
Use the dough hook of a hand mixer to process the ingredients thoroughly, first at low speed and then at full speed. Then knead the mixture on the work surface to form a smooth dough. Chill the dough for a while if it is sticky.
Roll out the dough on the base a 26-28 cm (11 inch) springform tin and prick several times with a fork. Put the springform rim around the base.

Oven temperatures
Conventional oven 200–220°C/400–425°F (preheated)
Fan-assisted oven about 170°C/325°F (not preheated)
Gas oven mark 3–4 (preheated)
Baking time about 15 minutes.

Loosen from the springform base immediately after baking. Allow to cool on the base and then transfer to a cake dish.

For the sponge mixture

4 eggs
100 g (3½ oz) sugar
2 tsp vanilla sugar

Use the whisk of a hand mixer to beat the eggs at full speed for 1 minute, until foaming. Combine the sugar and vanilla sugar and whisk into the eggs for 1 minute, then whisk for a further 2 minutes.

100 g (3½ oz) plain flour
25 g (1 oz) cornflour
1 tbsp cocoa powder
1 pinch ground cinnamon
½ tsp baking powder

Combine the flour, cornflour, cocoa powder, cinnamon and baking powder.

(continued on page 142)

Sieve half over the egg mixture and briefly whisk in at low speed. Work in the rest of the flour mixture in the same way.
Line a 26-28 cm (11 inch) springform tin with non-stick baking paper and grease the base. Pour the mixture into the tin and bake according to the instructions.

Oven temperatures
Conventional oven 170–200°C/375–400°F (preheated)
Fan-assisted oven –
Gas oven mark 3–4 (not preheated)
Baking time 25–30 minutes.

Loosen the cake from the tin, turn out and leave to cool.

For the filling

about 350 g (12 oz) canned cherries
or
500 g (1 lb 2 oz) red cherries
75 g (2¾ oz) sugar
2 tbsp cornflour
about 25 g (1 oz) sugar
about 3 tbsp kirsch
10 g (½ oz) unflavoured gelatine
5 tbsp cold water
750 ml (1¼ pints) double cream
40 g (1½ oz) icing sugar
2 tsp vanilla sugar

Drain the cherries, reserving the juice. If using fresh cherries, wash them, remove the stalks and stones, add 75 g (3 oz) sugar and leave for a while to draw out the juices. Bring to the boil, drain, keeping the juice, and leave to cool. Measure out 250 ml (9 fl oz) of the juice, topping up with water if necessary.
Mix the cornflour with 4 tablespoons of the juice and bring the rest of the juice to the boil. Remove the pan from the heat and stir in the cornflour mixture. Bring briefly to the boil and stir in the cherries. Leave to cool and add about 25 g (1 oz) sugar and 3 tablespoons of kirsch to taste.
Stir together the gelatine and water in a small pan and leave to soak for 10 minutes. Heat until the gelatine has dissolved, stirring continuously.
Whip the cream until almost stiff. Beat in the lukewarm gelatine solution and whip until completely stiff. Sieve the icing sugar, add the vanilla sugar and stir into the cream.

Spread the cherry mixture and a third of the cream over the pastry base (photo 1).
Cut the sponge into two layers and press the bottom layer firmly on top of the cream (photo 2). Spread with half the remaining cream and cover with the upper layer.

chocolate shavings
cherries
cream

Spread the remaining cream evenly over the top and sides and decorate the cake with chocolate shavings, cherries and cream, using a piping bag (photo 3).

Cranberry and Advocaat Cake

for special occasions

Preiselbeer-Eierlikör-Torte

For the sponge mixture

4 eggs
2 tbsp hot water
160 g (5¾ oz) sugar
2 tsp vanilla sugar
30 g (1 oz) plain flour
1 tsp baking powder

Use the whisk of a hand mixer to whisk the eggs and 2 tablespoons of hot water at full speed for 1 minute, until foamy. Combine the sugar and vanilla sugar and whisk in for 1 minute.
Combine the flour and baking powder. Sieve onto the egg mixture and briefly whisk in at low speed.

200 g (7 oz) ground hazelnuts
1 tsp ground cinnamon
60 g (2¼ oz) grated chocolate
50 g (2 oz) melted and cooled butter

Combine the ground hazelnuts and cinnamon and add to the mixture in the same way, together with the grated chocolate. Stir in the melted, slightly cooled butter.
Line a 26-28 cm (11 inch) springform tin with non-stick baking paper and grease the base. Pour the mixture into the tin and bake according to the instructions.

Oven temperatures

Conventional oven 170–200°C/375–400°F (preheated)
Fan-assisted oven –
Gas oven mark 3–4 (not preheated)
Baking time about 30 minutes.

Loosen the sponge from the tin, turn out and leave to cool.

For the topping

5–6 tbsp canned or stewed cranberries
500 ml (18 fl oz) double cream
2 tsp cream of tartar
2 tbsp sifted icing sugar
2 tsp vanilla sugar
250 ml (9 fl oz) advocaat

Spread the cranberries over the sponge, leaving 1 cm (½ inch) free at the edges. Whip the cream with the cream of tartar, icing sugar and vanilla sugar until stiff. Spread half the cream over the cranberries and place the rest in a piping bag with a star nozzle. Use this to decorate the sides of the cake.
Drizzle the advocaat over the cake and leave to cool for 3-4 hours.

Other red berries, such as redcurrants, could be used instead of cranberries.

Chocolate Orange Cake

Zaubertorte

fancy

For the sponge mixture

2 eggs
2 tbsp hot water
75 g (2¾ oz) sugar
2 tsp vanilla sugar

Use the whisk of a hand mixer to whisk the eggs and 2 tablespoons of hot water at full speed for 1 minute, until foamy. Combine the sugar and vanilla sugar and whisk for 1 minute, then whisk for a further 2 minutes.

75 g (2¾ oz) plain flour
½ tsp baking powder
50 g (2 oz) blanched, lightly toasted, ground almonds
50 g (2 oz) grated semi-sweet chocolate

Combine the flour and baking powder. Sift them over the egg mixture and add the toasted ground almonds and grated chocolate. Briefly whisk these ingredients in at low speed.

Line a 26-28 cm (11 inch) springform tin with non-stick baking paper and grease the base. Pour the mixture into the tin and bake according to the instructions.

Oven temperatures

Conventional oven 170–200°C/375-400°F (preheated)
Fan-assisted oven –
Gas oven mark 3–4 (not preheated)
Baking time about 25 minutes.

Loosen the sponge from the tin, turn out and leave to cool. Cut into two layers. Place the bottom layer on a cake plate, with the edge of the springform tin around it (lined with a strip of greaseproof or non-stick baking paper).

For the filling

10 g (½ oz) unflavoured gelatine
4 tbsp cold water
grated rind of ½ untreated orange
150 ml (¼ pint) orange juice
25 g (1 oz) sugar
50 g (2 oz) semi-sweet cooking chocolate

Combine the gelatine and water in a small pan and leave to soak for 10 minutes. Heat until the gelatine has dissolved, stirring continuously. Mix half the gelatine solution with the orange rind and juice and the sugar. Leave to cool.
Melt the chocolate in a bain-marie over a low heat until it is smooth, stirring continuously.

(continued on page 146)

500 ml (18 fl oz) double cream	Whip the cream until stiff and stir about two-thirds into the thickened orange juice. Spread the orange cream over the bottom layer, leaving some to decorate the top. Stir the cooled chocolate and remaining gelatine into the rest of the cream. Place the chocolate cream in a piping bag with a filling nozzle and pipe irregular dots over the orange cream, smoothing the surface if necessary. Place the upper layer on top and gently press together. Spread some of the remaining orange cream on top, decorate and chill to set the filling.
175 ml (6 fl oz) stiffly-whipped cream **30 g (1 oz) grated chocolate**	Carefully remove the springform rim from the cake, using a strip of greaseproof paper. Decorate the sides of the cake with whipped cream and sprinkle the grated chocolate on top.

Mandarin Omelettes

Mandarinenomeletts

for children

	For the moulds
30 cm (12 inch) aluminium foil	Fold a strip of aluminium foil 30 cm (12 inch) wide into seven strips on top of one another, each measuring 15 cm (6 inch) in length. Draw 2 circles, each of them 15 cm (6 inch) in diameter, next to one another and cut them out, creating 14 foil circles. Press these over the bottom of a tin about 10 cm (4 inch) in diameter, to obtain moulds about 2 cm (1 inch) high. Grease the insides of the moulds and place them on a baking sheet.
	For the sponge mixture
3 eggs **60 g (2½ oz) sugar** **2 tsp vanilla sugar**	Use the whisk of a hand mixer to whisk the eggs, sugar and vanilla sugar in a mixing bowl over boiling water. Whisk at full speed until the mixture is creamy. Remove the bowl from the bain-marie and continue to whisk until the mixture has cooled down.
50 g (2 oz) plain flour **50 g (2 oz) cornflour** **100 g (3½ oz) melted and cooled butter**	Combine the flour and cornflour, sift them and whisk into the egg mixture at low speed, alternating with the melted, slightly cooled butter. Divide the mixture between the moulds and bake immediately.

Oven temperatures	
Conventional oven	200–220°C/400–425°F (preheated)
Fan-assisted oven	–
Gas oven	mark 3–4 (preheated)
Baking time	10–15 minutes.
	Immediately remove the individual sponges from the moulds, fold them in half (over the handle of a wooden spoon is easiest) and leave to cool.
icing sugar	Dust lightly with icing sugar.

For the filling

2 tsp unflavoured gelatine	Stir together the gelatine and water in a small pan and leave to soak for 10 minutes.
3 tbsp cold water	
300 g (10½ oz) canned mandarins	Place the mandarin segments in a sieve to drain, reserving the juice.
375 ml (13 fl oz) double cream	Heat the gelatine until it has dissolved, stirring continuously.
2 tbsp lemon juice	Whip the cream until almost stiff. Add the lukewarm gelatine solution, lemon juice, mandarin juice, sugar and vanilla sugar.
2 tbsp mandarin juice	
2 tsp sugar	Whip the cream until completely stiff, pipe into the individual sponges and decorate with mandarin segments.
2 tsp vanilla sugar	

Tip Vary the filling. Use fresh fruit in season, such as redcurrants or raspberries, or fill the sponges with a chocolate cream.

Swiss Roll
Biskuitrolle

quick

3 eggs **5–6 tbsp hot water*** **150 g (5½ oz) sugar** **2 tsp vanilla sugar**	Use an electric whisk to beat the eggs with 5-6 tablespoons of hot water at full speed for 1 minute, until foaming. Combine the sugar and vanilla sugar and whisk in for 1 minute, then whisk for a further 2 minutes.
100 g (3½ oz) plain flour **50 g (2 oz) cornflour** **1 tsp baking powder**	Combine the flour, cornflour and baking powder. Sift half over the egg mixture and briefly whisk in at low speed. Work in the rest of the flour mixture in the same way.
	Pour the mixture onto a greased baking sheet or Swiss roll tin lined with non-stick baking paper to a depth of about 1 cm (½ inch). If the baking sheet has an open side, fold the paper directly in front of the mixture to form an edge (photo 1). Bake immediately.
Oven temperatures	
Conventional oven	200–220°C/400–425°F (preheated)
Fan-assisted oven	–
Gas oven	mark 3–4 (preheated)
Baking time	10–15 minutes.
sugar **250-375 g (9-13 oz) jam** **30 g (1 oz) icing sugar**	Immediately after baking, turn the sponge out onto a tea towel sprinkled with sugar. Brush the paper with cold water and quickly but carefully remove the paper. Immediately brush the jam evenly over the sponge (photo 2) and roll it up from the shortest side (photo 3). Dust with icing sugar.

* Use less water for large eggs and more water for small eggs.

Buttercream Cake

Buttercremetorte

suitable for freezing

For the sponge mixture

4 eggs
2-4 tbsp hot water*
150 g (5½ oz) sugar
2 tsp vanilla sugar

Use the whisk of a hand mixer to whisk the eggs and 2-4 tablespoons of hot water at full speed for 1 minute, until foaming. Combine the sugar and vanilla sugar and whisk in for 1 minute, then whisk for a further 2 minutes.

100 g (3½ oz) plain flour
100 g (3½ oz) cornflour
2 tsp baking powder

Combine the flour, cornflour and baking powder. Sieve half onto the egg mixture and briefly whisk in at low speed. Work in the rest of the flour mixture in the same way.

Line a 26-28 cm (11 inch) springform tin with non-stick baking paper and grease the base. Pour the mixture into the tin and bake according to the instructions.

Oven temperatures	
Conventional oven	170–200°C/375–400°F (preheated)
Fan-assisted oven	–
Gas oven	mark 3–4 (not preheated)
Baking time	20–30 minutes.

Loosen the sponge from the tin, turn out and leave to cool.

For the chocolate buttercream

1 packet chocolate pudding powder
25 g (1 oz) sugar
500 ml (18 fl oz) milk
100 g (3½ oz) semi-sweet cooking chocolate

Make the chocolate pudding according to the packet directions, adding the milk but not using more than 25 g (1 oz) sugar.
Break the chocolate into small pieces and add to the hot dessert mixture. Stir until the chocolate has melted. Leave to cool, stirring occasionally,

or

for light buttercream

1 packet vanilla, almond or caramel pudding powder
75-100 g (2¾-3½ oz) sugar
500 ml (18 fl oz) milk

Make the vanilla, almond or caramel dessert according to the instructions on the packet, adding the milk but not using more than 75-100 g (3-3½ oz) sugar. Leave to cool, stirring occasionally,

or

for mocha buttercream

1 packet chocolate pudding powder
75-100 g (2¾-3½ oz) sugar
1 tbsp instant coffee
500 ml (18 fl oz) milk
250 g (9 oz) butter

Make the chocolate dessert according to the instructions on the packet, adding the instant coffee and milk but not using more than 75-100 g (3-3½ oz) sugar. Leave to cool, stirring occasionally. Cream the butter and add to the cooled dessert mixture a tablespoon at a time. Make sure that neither the butter nor the dessert are too cold, as the mixture will coagulate.

chocolate strands or blanched, slivered, toasted almonds

Cut the cake into three layers and spread a quarter of the buttercream over the bottom layer (if required, first brush this layer with 2-3 tablespoons of jam). Place the second layer on top and spread with no more than half the remaining buttercream. Place the third layer on top. Spread some of the remaining buttercream thinly and evenly over the top and sides of the cake, and sprinkle the chocolate flakes or almonds over the sides.
Decorate with the remaining cream and finish as required with chocolate strands or toasted almonds.

Tip For a light-coloured buttercream cake, you could also use the dark Victoria sponge base (see basic recipe on page 137).

* Use less water for large eggs and more water for small eggs.

Mocha Cream Cake

traditional

Mokka-Sahne-Torte

For the sponge mixture

- 3 eggs
- 3 tbsp hot water
- 150 g (5½ oz) sugar
- 2 tsp vanilla sugar
- 100 g (3½ oz) plain flour
- 100 g (3½ oz) cornflour
- 3 tsp baking powder

Use an electric whisk to beat the eggs with 3 tablespoons of hot water at full speed for 1 minute, until foaming. Mix together the sugar and vanilla sugar and whisk in for 1 minute, then whisk for a further 2 minutes.

Mix together the flour, cornflour and baking powder. Sift half over the egg mixture and briefly whisk in at low speed. Work in the rest of the flour mixture in the same way.

Line a 26-28 cm (11 inch) springform tin with non-stick baking paper and grease the base. Pour the mixture into the tin and bake according to the instructions.

Oven temperatures	
Conventional oven	170–200°C/400°F (preheated)
Fan-assisted oven	–
Gas oven	mark 3–4 (not preheated)
Baking time	20–30 minutes.

Loosen the sponge from the tin, turn out and leave to cool.

For the filling

- 3 tsp instant coffee granules
- 150 ml (5 fl oz) cold water
- 750 ml (1¼ pints) double cream
- 1 packet instant topping
- 1 tbsp orange liqueur
- 2 tbsp apricot jam

Dissolve the instant coffee in the cold water. Whip the cream with the instant topping and beat in the coffee solution.

Cut the cake into two layers. Sprinkle the orange liqueur over the bottom layer, then spread with apricot jam and pile two-thirds of the cream mixture on top (photo 1).

(continued on page 154)

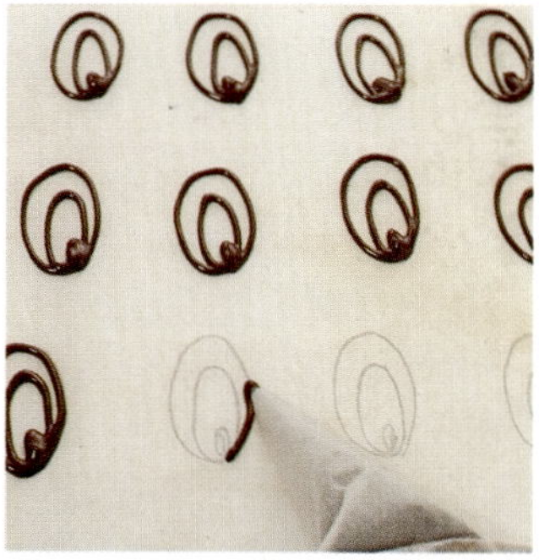

Place the top layer on the cream mixture and press down firmly. Pile the rest of the cream mixture over the cake and make depressions with a tablespoon (photo 2). Leave to cool.

To decorate

50 g (2 oz) semi-sweet chocolate cake covering	Place the chocolate cake covering in a small pan. Stir at low heat over a bain-marie until smooth. Pipe shapes on non-stick baking paper (photo 3) and leave to set. Decorate the cake with the chocolate shapes and dust with cocoa powder.
cocoa powder	Cut into 16 slices.

Lemon Cream Roll

popular

Zitronen-Sahne-Rolle

For the sponge mixture

4 eggs	Use the whisk of a hand mixer to whisk the eggs and
3-4 tbsp hot water	3-4 tablespoons of hot water at full speed for 1 minute, until
125 g (4½ oz) sugar	foaming . Mix together the sugar and vanilla sugar and whisk in
1 tsp vanilla sugar	for 1 minute, then whisk for a further 2 minutes.
75 g (2¾ oz) plain flour	Mix together the flour, cornflour and baking powder. Sieve half
50 g (1¾ oz) cornflour	over the egg mixture and briefly whisk in at low speed. Work in
1 pinch baking powder	the rest of the flour mixture in the same way.

Pour the mixture into a greased baking sheet or Swiss roll tin lined with non-stick baking paper, to a depth of about 1 cm (½ inch). At the open side of the baking sheet, fold the paper directly in front of the mixture to form an edge. Bake immediately.

Oven temperatures	
Conventional oven	200–220°C/400–425°F (preheated)
Fan-assisted oven	–
Gas oven	mark 3–4 (preheated)
Baking time	10–15 minutes.

sugar — Immediately after baking, turn the sponge out on to a tea towel sprinkled with sugar. Brush the paper with cold water and quickly but carefully remove the paper. Use the tea towel to roll up the sponge from the shortest side and leave to cool.

For the filling

2 tsp unflavoured gelatine
2 tbsp cold water
3 sugar cubes
rind of 1/2 untreated lemon
5 tbsp lemon juice
500 ml (18 fl oz) double cream

Combine the gelatine and water in a small pan and leave to soak for 10 minutes. Use the corners of the sugar cubes to rub the rind of half a lemon. Heat the soaked gelatine with the sugar cubes until both ingredients have dissolved, stirring continuously. Add the lemon juice.
Whip the cream until almost stiff and beat in the lukewarm gelatine solution. Whip the cream until completely stiff.

Carefully unroll the cooled sponge and spread with two-thirds of the lemon cream. Roll it up again, removing the thin brown crust on the outside. Then spread a thin layer of lemon cream over the roll, followed by the rest of the lemon cream. Use a fork to mark wavy lines along the length of the roll.

* Use less water for large eggs and more water for small eggs.

Punch Cake

Punschtorte

for special occasions

You will need to make two quantities of sponge mixture for this recipe.

For the cake (quantities for each sponge layer)

4 eggs
3–4 tbsp hot water *
150 g (5½ oz) sugar
2 tsp vanilla sugar

Use an electric whisk to whisk the eggs and 3-4 tablespoons of hot water at full speed for 1 minute, until foaming . Mix together the sugar and vanilla sugar and whisk in for 1 minute, then whisk for a further 2 minutes.

100 g (3½ oz) plain flour
100 g (3½ oz) cornflour
3 tsp baking powder

Mix together the flour, cornflour and baking powder. Sift half the dry ingredients over the egg mixture and briefly whisk in at low speed. Work in the rest of the flour mixture in the same way. Line a 26-28 cm (11 inch) springform tin with non-stick baking paper and grease the base. Pour the mixture into the tin and bake according to the instructions.

Oven temperatures	
Conventional oven	180–200 °C/350–400°F (preheated)
Fan-assisted oven	–
Gas oven	mark 3–4 (not preheated)
Baking time	20–30 minutes.

Make two sponge bases, turn out and leave to cool.

For the filling

8 sugar lumps
rind of one untreated orange
8 tbsp orange juice
2-3 tbsp lemon juice
200 ml (7 fl oz) sweet red wine
6 tbsp rum

Crumble one of the sponge bases. Use the corners of the sugar cubes to rub off the rind of the orange and heat the chocolate with the sugar cubes, orange juice, lemon juice, red wine and rum.

(continued on page 158)

50 g (2 oz) semi-sweet chocolate
200 g (7 oz) redcurrant jelly

Immediately stir the melted chocolate into the crumbs.

Cut a layer at least 1 cm (½ inch) thick from the top of the other sponge base. Brush the bottom layer with some of the redcurrant jelly and spread the filling on top. Brush some more redcurrant jelly over the filling and press the upper layer firmly on top (photo 1). Brush the rest of the redcurrant jelly over the top and sides of the cake.

100 g (3½ oz) sifted icing sugar
200 g (7 oz) marzipan

Knead the icing sugar into the marzipan and roll out until about 2 mm (1/16 inch) thick (photo 2). Cut out a strip the same height as the sides of the cake and a circle to fit the top.
Place the marzipan on and around the cake (photo 3) and press firmly into position.

For the icing

100 g (3½ oz) sifted icing sugar
about 2 tbsp mallow tea (made from one 1 teabag steeped in 4 tbsp boiling water)
about 6 glacé cherries, halved
50 g (2 oz) icing sugar
hot water
beetroot juice

Combine the sifted icing sugar and mallow tea until a thick cream is obtained. Cover the cake with the mixture and decorate with the halved glacé cherries. If required, stir together 50 g (2 oz) icing sugar and a little hot water and beetroot juice and drizzle over the cake.

If mallow tea is not available, use rosehip or hibiscus tea.

* Use less water for large eggs and more water for small eggs.

No-bake Cheesecake

Blitz-Käsetorte

popular

For the base

150 g (5½ oz) sponge fingers
120 g (4 oz) margarine or butter

Put the sponge fingers in a plastic bag, close the bag and crush the sponge fingers with a rolling pin. Put the crumbs in a bowl. Melt the margarine or butter and add to the crumbs. Stir well.

Line a 26-28 cm (11 inch) springform tin with non-stick baking paper and grease the base. Pour the crumbs into the tin and spread evenly.

For the filling

1 sachet lemon jelly crystals
200 ml (7 fl oz) water

Combine the lemon jelly crystals and water and leave to soak for 10 minutes. Heat, stirring continuously, until the jelly has dissolved. Leave to cool slightly.

200 g (7 oz) double cream soft cheese (such as mascarpone)
125 g (4½ oz) sugar
2 tsp vanilla sugar
2 tbsp lemon juice
500 ml (18 fl oz) stiffly whipped cream

Stir together the cream cheese and sugar, vanilla sugar and lemon juice. Add the lukewarm jelly. When the mixture begins to thicken, fold in the whipped cream and spread the cheesecake mixture over the base, smoothing the surface.

For the topping

30 g (1 oz) sponge fingers

Crumble the sponge fingers and sprinkle them over the cheesecake mixture. Serve chilled.
Place a springform ring on a cake dish and press the base mixture firmly into the ring.

Tip Decorate the cheesecake with tinned mandarin segments or pineapple pieces, as required.

Carrot - Nut Cake

Möhren-Nuß-Torte

fancy

For the sponge mixture

- 6 eggs
- 3 tbsp lemon juice
- 300 g (10½ oz) sugar
- 2 tsp vanilla sugar
- 100 g (3½ oz) plain flour
- 1 pinch baking powder
- grated rind of an untreated lemon
- 600 g (1 lb 5 oz) grated carrot
- 100 g (3½ oz) ground hazelnuts
- 300 g (10½ oz) chopped hazelnuts

Use the whisk of a hand mixer to whisk the eggs and the lemon juice at full speed for 1 minute, until foaming. Mix together the sugar and vanilla sugar and whisk in for 1 minute, then whisk for a further 2 minutes.

Mix together the flour and baking powder. Sift half over the egg mixture and briefly whisk in at low speed. Work in the rest of the flour mixture in the same way. Fold in the grated lemon rind, finely grated carrots and the ground and chopped hazelnuts.

Line a 26-28 cm (11 inch) springform tin with non-stick baking paper and grease the base. Pour the mixture into the tin and bake immediately.

Oven temperatures	
Conventional oven	170–200 °C/350–400°F (preheated)
Fan-assisted oven	–
Gas oven	mark 3–4 (not preheated)
Baking time	about 1 hour.

Loosen the sponge from the tin, turn out and leave to cool.

For the apricot glaze

- 100 g (3½ oz) apricot jam (sieved)
- 3½ tbsp water

Press the apricot jam through a sieve and bring briefly to the boil with 3 generous tablespoons of water, stirring continuously. Brush over the cake.

For the marzipan coating

- 200 g (7 oz) marzipan
- 50 g (2 oz) sifted icing sugar
- additional icing sugar for the work surface

Knead the sifted icing sugar into the marzipan. Dust the work surface with icing sugar and thinly roll out the marzipan. Cut out a circle for the top and a strip measuring the same height as the sides. Place the marzipan over and around the cake

For the icing

- 250 g (9 oz) icing sugar
- about 4 tbsp lemon juice
- marzipan carrots

Stir together the sieved icing sugar and the lemon juice until a thick mixture is obtained. Cover the cake with the mixture and decorate with marzipan carrots if required.

Serving suggestion Serve with slightly sweetened whipped cream.

Lüneburg Buckwheat Cake

traditional

Lüneburger Buchweizentorte

For the sponge mixture

5 eggs	Use an electric whisk to beat the eggs and 2 tablespoons of hot
2 tbsp hot water	water at full speed for 1 minute, until foaming. Mix together the
150 g (5½ oz) sugar	sugars and whisk in for 1 minute, then whisk for a further
2 tsp muscovado sugar	2 minutes.
3 drops almond essence	Stir in the almond essence.
150 g (5½ oz) buckwheat flour	Combine the buckwheat flour and baking powder. Sift half over
1 tsp baking powder	the egg mixture and briefly whisk in at low speed (photo 1).
100 g (3½ oz) finely ground hazelnuts	Work in the rest of the flour and the ground hazelnuts in the same way.
	Line a 26-28 cm (11 inch) springform tin with non-stick baking paper and grease the base. Pour the mixture into the tin and bake immediately.
Oven temperature	
Conventional oven	170–200 °C/350–400°F (preheated)
Fan-assisted oven	–
Gas oven	mark 3–4 (not preheated)
Baking time	about 30 minutes.
	Loosen the sponge from the tin, turn out and leave to cool.

For the filling

175 g (6 oz) canned cranberries, drained	Leave the cranberry dessert to drain and measure out 350 ml (12 fl oz) of the juice. Prepare the jelly glaze using the juice and
2 packets red jelly glaze	sugar and following the instructions on the packet. Stir in the
30 g (2 tbsp) sugar	cranberries (photo 2) and bring briefly to the boil once again. Leave to cool.
3 tsp unflavoured gelatine	Stir together the gelatine and water in a small pan and leave to
3 tbsp cold water	soak for 10 minutes. Heat the gelatine until it has dissolved, stirring continuously.

(continued on page 164)

600 ml (1 pint) double cream **2 tsp vanilla sugar**	Whip the cream and the vanilla sugar until almost stiff and beat in the lukewarm gelatine solution. Whip the cream until completely stiff.
	Cut the cake into three layers and spread a third of the cranberry mixture over the bottom layer. Spread about 3 tablespoons of the cream on top and cover with the middle layer. Spread the cranberry mixture and cream over the middle layer as before and place the upper layer on top (photo 3).
ground pistachio nuts	Spread cream over the top and sides of the cake and make patterns on the sides. Place the rest of the cream in a piping bag with a star nozzle and decorate the cake. Finish with the rest of the cranberry mixture and ground pistachios.
Tip	The cake tastes best if it is made the previous day and refrigerated.
Variation	Use 350 g (12 oz) plum jam instead of the cranberry filling.

Sponge fingers
Löffelbiskuits

for children

2 eggs **50 g (2 oz) sugar** **2 tsp vanilla sugar** **50 g (1¾ oz) plain flour** **30 g (1 oz) cornflour** **1 tsp baking powder**	Use the whisk of a hand mixer to whisk the eggs, sugar and vanilla sugar at full speed for 2 minutes, until creamy. Mix together the flour, cornflour and baking powder. Sift over the egg mixture and briefly whisk in at low speed. Place the mixture in a piping bag with a plain nozzle and pipe sponge fingers onto a greased baking sheet lightly dusted with flour. Do not make them too big, as they will rise during baking. Bake immediately.
Oven temperatures	
Conventional oven	180–200°C/350–400°F (preheated)
Fan-assisted oven	–
Gas oven	mark 2–3 (preheated)
Baking time	about 10 minutes.
icing sugar	Dust the cooled sponge fingers with icing sugar.

Langues de Chat

Mandelzungen

quick

For the sponge mixture

- 3 egg whites
- 125 g (4½ oz) sugar
- 2 tbsp plain flour
- 1 tsp cocoa powder
- 100 g (3½ oz) unblanched, ground almonds
- 60 g (2½ oz) melted and cooled margarine or butter

Use an electric whisk to whisk the egg whites at full speed until almost stiff. Gradually whisk in the sugar. Mix together the flour and cocoa powder and sieve onto the egg whites. Fold in. Whisk in the ground almonds at low speed. Stir in the melted, cooled margarine or butter and place the almond mixture in a piping bag with a plain nozzle. Pipe 3-4 cm (1½ inch) lengths on a greased baking sheet lined with non-stick baking paper.

Oven temperatures	
Conventional oven	170–200 °C/375–400°F (preheated)
Fan-assisted oven	–
Gas oven	mark 3–4 (preheated)
Baking time	about 12 minutes.

Loosen the biscuits from the baking sheet immediately after baking.

For the filling

- about 100 g (3½ oz) chocolate spread

Stir the chocolate in a small pan over a bain-marie, at low heat, until smooth. Spread half the almond tongues with the mixture and place the remaining biscuits on top.

For the icing

- 50 g (2 oz) chocolate cake covering

Stir the cake covering in a small pan over a bain-marie, at low heat, until smooth. Dip the ends of the biscuits into the glaze and leave to dry on non-stick baking paper. Store in tightly sealed tins.

Advocaat cake

quick

Eierlikörkuchen

5 eggs
250 g (9 oz) sifted icing sugar
4 tsp vanilla sugar
250 ml (9 fl oz) vegetable oil
250 ml (9 fl oz) Advocaat
125 g (4½ oz) plain flour
125 g (4½ oz) cornflour
4 tsp baking powder
flour for dusting

Use the whisk of a hand mixer to whisk the eggs, icing sugar and vanilla sugar at full speed for 1 minute, until foaming . Whisk in the oil and Advocaat (photo 1).
Mix together the flour, cornflour and baking powder. Sift and whisk into the egg mixture in portions at medium speed.
Grease a 24 cm (9½ inch) greased ring mould and dust with flour. Turn the mixture into it (photo 2) and bake immediately.

Oven temperature
Conventional oven 170–200°C/350–400°F (preheated)
Fan-assisted oven –
Gas oven mark 3–4 (not preheated)
Baking time about 1 hour.

Leave the cake in the mould for about 10 minutes, turn out and leave to cool.

40 g (1½ oz) icing sugar

Dust with icing sugar.

Variation

Advocaat waffles

2 eggs
100 g (3½ oz) icing sugar
2 tsp vanilla sugar
100 ml (3½ fl oz) vegetable oil
100 ml (3½ fl oz) Advocaat
50 g (2 oz) plain flour
50 g (2 oz) cornflour
1 ½ tsp baking powder

Prepare the sponge mixture as above, using the eggs, icing sugar, vanilla sugar, oil, Advocaat, flour, cornflour and baking powder.

For each waffle, place 3 tablespoons of the mixture in a well-heated, greased waffle iron (photo 3) and bake until golden.

Prophet cake

Prophetenkuchen

quick

For the sponge mixture

6 egg yolks
100 ml (3½ fl oz) vegetable oil
100 ml (3½ fl oz) rum (40° proof)
100 g (3½ oz) plain flour

Use an electric whisk to whisk the egg yolks for 5 minutes at full speed, until foaming. Briefly whisk in the oil and the rum (photo 1). Sift the flour and whisk in at medium speed for 1 minute.
Whisk the mixture again for a short time at full speed and spread on a well-greased baking sheet (photo 2).

Oven temperatures	
Conventional oven	about 250°C/475°F (preheated)
Fan-assisted oven	–
Gas oven	mark 4–5 (preheated)
Baking time	about 7 minutes.

Leave the cake to cool on the baking sheet.

For the topping

100 g (3½ oz) butter
4 tsp vanilla sugar
100 g (3½ oz) icing sugar

Melt the butter and brush over the cake (photo 3). Sprinkle with the vanilla sugar. When the butter has set, dust with the icing sugar.

Tip The cake should only be baked until golden. Make sure that you use rum that is 40° proof.

Preparation required

Mix and sift the flour and baking powder.
Mixing and sifting breaks up the flour and distributes the baking powder evenly throughout the flour. This makes the cake much lighter.

For quark and oil dough, grease the baking sheets and tins.
It is best to use spreadable margarine or butter, spread thoroughly and evenly with a pastry brush.

The individual steps

The flour (which has been mixed with baking powder and sifted), quark, milk and, depending on the recipe, egg, oil, sugar (honey), vanilla sugar and salt are combined using the dough hook of a hand mixer at full speed for about 1 minute.
Add the ingredients to the mixing bowl in the specified order. Each egg should first be broken into a cup to check for freshness.
With this type of dough, the oil is extremely important and must not be replaced with solid fat. Any oil with a neutral taste can be used.

Dust your hands with flour and shape the dough into a roll on the work surface.
If the dough is too soft, add a little more flour. Make sure you do not add too much, or the texture of the cake will be dry.
This dough can be used for the a wide variety of

cakes and pastries. It can be rolled out, shaped, filled or iced as required. To make biscuits, roll the dough out until it is at least 5 mm (¼ inch) thick, cut it into squares and spread a little jam in the centre. Fold the squares to form triangles, pockets, etc., brush with milk and bake on a greased baking sheet.

Basic recipe

Grundrezept

300-400 g (10½ - 14 oz) plain flour
1 tbsp- 1½ tbsp baking powder
150-200 g (5½ - 7 oz) low-fat quark
6 tbsp milk
6-8 tbsp vegetable oil
75-100 g (3-3½ oz) sugar
2 tsp vanilla sugar
1 egg (optional)
1 pinch salt
sweet spices (optional)

Mix together the flour and the baking powder and sift into a mixing bowl. Add the quark, milk, oil, sugar, vanilla sugar, egg (if used), salt and spices (if used).
Use the dough hook of a hand mixer to work the mixture into a dough at full speed for about 1 minute (not too long or the dough will be sticky).
Then shape the dough into a roll on the floured work surface.
Process and bake as specified in the recipe.

Baking quark and oil dough

All types of quark and oil dough should be baked according to the instructions in the recipe. After baking, immediately turn out from the tin or remove from the baking sheet and place on a wire rack to cool. Cakes or pastries made from quark -and-oil dough are best eaten as fresh as possible.

Orange and marzipan plaits

easy

Orangen-Marzipan-Zöpfchen **(see photo on pages 170/171)**

For the filling

- 200 g (7 oz) marzipan
- 50 g (2 oz) softened margarine or butter
- 2 tbsp sieved orange marmalade

Use the whisk of a hand mixer to beat together the marzipan, softened margarine or butter and the marmalade.

For the dough

- 300 g (10½ oz) plain flour
- 15 g (1 tbsp) baking powder
- 150 g (5½ oz) low-fat quark
- 100 ml (3½ fl oz) milk
- 100 ml (3½ fl oz) vegetable oil
- 80 g (3 oz) sugar
- 2 tsp vanilla sugar
- 1 pinch salt
- 1 egg white, lightly beaten

Combine the flour and the baking powder and sift into a mixing bowl. Add the quark, milk, oil, sugar, vanilla sugar and salt.
Use the dough hook of a hand mixer to work the mixture into a dough at full speed for about 1 minute (not too long or the dough will be sticky).
Shape the dough into a roll on the floured work surface.
Roll out the dough into a rectangle measuring about 36 x 48 cm (14 x 19 inch) and cut it into 12 x 12 cm (5 x 5 inch) squares.
Spread some of the filling on to half of each square, leaving ½-1 cm (½ inch) free at the edges. Brush the edges with the beaten egg white and fold the other half of each square over the filling. Press down gently.
Make two lengthways cuts along each piece, stopping 1 cm (½ inch) before the top edge. Plait the three connected dough strips and press the ends gently together.

- 1 egg yolk
- 1 tbsp milk

Arrange the little plaits on a baking sheet lined with non-stick baking paper. Beat the egg yolk with the milk and brush it over the plaits before baking.

Oven temperatures

Conventional oven	170–200°C/350–400°F (preheated)
Fan-assisted oven	160–170°C/350°F (not preheated)
Gas oven	mark 3–4 (preheated)
Baking time	15–20 minutes.

For the icing

- 100 g (3½ oz) sifted icing sugar
- 1-2 tbsp orange juice

Combine the sifted icing sugar and the orange juice until a thick mixture is obtained. Ice the plaits immediately after baking.

Marzipan and raisin pinwheels

Gerollte Schnitten

150 g (5½ oz) plain flour
4 tsp baking powder
75 g (3 oz) low-fat quark
50 ml (2 fl oz) milk
50 ml (2 fl oz) vegetable oil
40 g (1½ oz) sugar
2 tsp vanilla sugar
½ tsp butterscotch essence
1 pinch salt

For the dough

Mix together the flour and the baking powder and sift into a mixing bowl. Add the quark, milk, oil, sugar, vanilla sugar, butterscotch flavouring and salt.

Use the dough hook of a hand mixer to work the mixture into a dough at full speed for about 1 minute (not too long or the dough will be sticky).

Then shape the dough into a roll on the floured work surface.

100 g (3½ oz) marzipan
50 g (2 oz) margarine or butter
1 egg yolk
125 g (4½ oz) raisins
50 g (2 oz) chopped hazelnuts
25 g (1 oz) candied citron or lemon peel, finely chopped
1 pinch ground cinnamon
½ tsp rum essence

For the filling

Use an electric whisk to beat together the marzipan, margarine or butter and egg yolk until smooth.

Combine the raisins, chopped hazelnuts, candied peel, cinnamon and rum flavouring.

Roll out the dough on the lightly floured work surface to form a 30 x 30 cm (12 x 12 inch) square. Spread the marzipan mixture on top. Scatter the raisin mixture over the top and gently press into the marzipan. Roll up the dough and place on a baking sheet lined with non-stick baking paper. Make a longitudinal cut of about 25 cm (10 inch) and about 2½ cm (1 inch) deep. Pull the roll apart slightly and press the sides together again.

Oven temperatures

Conventional oven	170–200°C /350–400°F (preheated)
Fan-assisted oven	about 160°C/325°F (not preheated)
Gas oven	mark 3–4 (preheated)
Baking time	25–35 minutes.

80 g (3 oz) icing sugar
1-2 tbsp rum

For the icing

Sift the icing sugar and stir in the rum until a thick mixture is obtained. Ice the plaits immediately after baking. Leave the icing to set and cut into slices 1-2 cm (½ inch) wide.

Quark and redcurrant cake with meringue

for guests

Johannisbeer-Quark-Kuchen mit Baiser

For the dough

- 300 g (10½ oz) plain flour
- 15 g (1 tbsp) baking powder
- 150 g (5½ oz) low-fat quark
- 100 ml (3½ fl oz) milk
- 100 ml (3½ fl oz) vegetable oil
- 75 g (3 oz) sugar
- 2 tsp vanilla sugar
- 1 pinch salt

Combine the flour and the baking powder and sift into a mixing bowl. Add the quark, milk, oil, sugar, vanilla sugar and salt (photo 1).

Use the dough hook of a hand mixer to work the mixture into a dough at full speed for about 1 minute (not too long or the dough will be sticky).

Then shape the dough into a roll on the floured work surface. Roll out the dough on a greased baking sheet until it is no more than ½ cm (¼ inch) thick (the dough should cover about three-quarters of the baking sheet). Place a pleated strip of aluminium foil in front of the dough.

For the topping

- 500-750 g (1lb 2 oz-1lb 10 oz) redcurrants
- 750 g (1lb 10 oz) low-fat quark
- 200 g (7 oz) sugar
- 2 tsp vanilla sugar
- 3 eggs
- 2 egg yolks
- 50 g (2 oz) softened margarine or butter
- 50 g (2 oz) cornflour

Wash the redcurrants and drain thoroughly. Remove the stalks. Combine the quark, sugar, vanilla sugar, eggs, egg yolks, softened margarine or butter and cornflour. Fold the redcurrants into the quark mixture and spread it over the dough (photo 2). Smooth the surface.

(continued on page 178)

Oven temperatures	
Conventional oven	170–200°C/375–400°F (preheated)
Fan-assisted oven	160–170°C/325°F (not preheated)
Gas oven	mark 3–4 (preheated)
Baking time	about 25 minutes.

For the meringue

2 egg whites
100 g (3½ oz) sugar
4 tsp blanched, slivered almonds

Whisk the egg whites until stiff. They must be sufficiently stiff to retain a trail left by the edge of a knife. Gradually beat in the sugar a tablespoon at a time. Spread the meringue mixture over the quark topping (photo 3). Sprinkle the almonds on top.

Oven temperatures	
Conventional oven	200–220°C/400–425°F (preheated)
Fan-assisted oven	170–190°C/350°F (not preheated)
Gas oven	mark 4–5 (preheated)
Baking time	about 5 minutes.

Kirsch cream cake

for children

Kirsch-Sahne-Torte

For the dough

150 g (5½ oz) plain flour
4 tsp baking powder
2 tsp cocoa powder
75 g (3 oz) low-fat quark
100 ml (3½ fl oz) milk
50 ml (2 fl oz) vegetable oil
40 g (1½ oz) sugar
2 tsp vanilla sugar
50 ml (2 fl oz) butterscotch flavouring
1 pinch salt

Combine the flour, baking powder and cocoa powder and sift into a mixing bowl. Add the quark, milk, oil, sugar, vanilla sugar, butterscotch flavouring and salt.
Use the dough hook of a hand mixer to work the mixture into a dough at full speed for about 1 minute (not too long or the dough will be sticky).
Then shape the dough into a roll on the floured work surface.
Grease the base of a 28 cm (11 inch) springform tin and line it with non-stick baking paper. Place the dough in the tin.

For the filling

350 g (12 oz) canned red cherries

Place the cherries in a sieve to drain. Keep the juice and measure out 250 ml (9 fl oz).
Spread the cherries over the dough, leaving 1 cm (½ inch) free at the edge.

Oven temperatures	
Conventional oven	about 170°C/350°F (preheated)
Fan-assisted oven	about 150°C/300°F (not preheated)
Gas oven	mark 3 (not preheated)
Baking time	about 25 minutes.

Remove the cake from the tin and leave to cool on a wire rack. Place the cooled cake on a cake plate, with the edge of the spring-form tin around the cake.

For the topping

500 ml (18 fl oz) double cream
1 tbsp cream of tartar
4 tsp sifted icing sugar

Whip the cream for 30 seconds. Mix the cream of tartar with the sifted icing sugar and sprinkle over the cream. Whip the cream until stiff and spread evenly over the cake.

For the glaze

1 packet clear jelly glaze
1 tbsp sugar
250 ml (9 fl oz) cherry juice

Prepare the glaze according to the instructions on the packet, using the sugar and the cherry juice. Immediately pour over the cream, forming a pattern.

Tip If using fresh cherries, wash 500 g (1 lb 2 oz) sour cherries and remove the stalks and stones. Mix with 50 g (2 oz) sugar and leave for a short time to draw out the juices. Bring briefly to the boil and leave to drain. When the juice and cherries are both cold, measure out 250 ml (9 fl oz) of the juice (top up with water if necessary).

Crumb Quark Apple Cake

simple

Quark-Apfel-Kuchen mit Streuseln

For the dough

300 g ($10\frac{1}{2}$ oz) plain flour
15 g (1 tbsp) baking powder
150 g ($5\frac{1}{2}$ oz) low-fat quark
100 ml ($3\frac{1}{2}$ fl oz) milk
100 ml ($3\frac{1}{2}$ fl oz) vegetable oil
75 g (3 oz) sugar
2 tsp vanilla sugar
1 pinch salt

Combine the flour and the baking powder and sift into a mixing bowl. Add the quark, milk, oil, sugar, vanilla sugar and salt.
Use the dough hook of a hand mixer to work the mixture into a dough at full speed for about 1 minute (not too long or the dough will be sticky).

Then shape the dough into a roll on the floured work surface. Roll out the dough on a greased baking sheet and place a folded strip of aluminium foil in front of the dough if one side of the baking sheet is open.

For the topping

$1\frac{1}{2}$ kg (3 lb 5 oz) cooking apples
150 g ($5\frac{1}{2}$ oz) margarine or butter
100 g ($3\frac{1}{2}$ oz) sugar
$\frac{1}{4}$ tsp lemon essence
4 egg yolks
850 g (1 lb 14 oz) low-fat quark
50 g (2 oz) semolina
4 egg whites

Peel, quarter, core and thinly slice the apples. Arrange the slices on the dough so that they overlap.

Cream the margarine or butter and the sugar and gradually stir in the lemon essence, egg yolks, quark and semolina. Whisk the egg whites until stiff and fold into the quark mixture. Spread over the apples.

For the crumble topping

200 g (7 oz) plain flour
70 g ($2\frac{1}{2}$ oz) blanched, ground almonds
150 g ($5\frac{1}{2}$ oz) sugar
$\frac{1}{2}$ tsp ground cinnamon
1 egg yolk
150-200 g ($5\frac{1}{2}$-7 oz) margarine or butter

Sift the flour into a bowl and mix with the ground almonds, sugar, cinnamon, egg yolk and margarine or butter. Use the dough hook of a hand mixer to beat the mixture until it resembles coarse breadcrumbs. Sprinkle it evenly over the quark mixture.

Oven temperatures	
Conventional oven	about 170°C/325°F (preheated)
Fan-assisted oven	about 150°C/300°F (not preheated)
Gas oven	about mark 3 (preheated)
Baking time	about 1 hour.

Tip This cake tastes best served lukewarm, with cream if required.

Variations

50 g (2 oz) blanched, slivered almonds	Instead of the crumble topping, sprinkle the slivered almonds and raisins over the quark mixture
50 g (2 oz) raisins	
	or
	instead of the apples,
950 g (2lb 2 oz) canned apricots	
or	canned apricots or gooseberries may also be used instead of the apples. Drain the apricots or gooseberries in a siftand spread them over the dough.
800 g (1lb 12 oz) canned gooseberries	

Hazelnut Plait

Haselnußzopf

traditional

For the filling

100 g (3½ oz) ground hazelnuts 100 g (3½ oz) marzipan 1 egg 2 tbsp sugar 2 tsp vanilla sugar 1 tsp rum essence	Lightly toast the ground hazelnuts in a dry frying pan, stirring continuously. Leave to cool. Beat the marzipan with the egg, sugar, vanilla sugar and rum essence until smooth. Stir in the hazelnuts.

For the dough

300 g (10½ oz) plain flour 15 g (1 tbsp) baking powder 150 g (5½ oz) low-fat quark 100 ml (3½ fl oz) milk 100 ml (3½ fl oz) vegetable oil 80 g (3 oz) sugar 2 tsp vanilla sugar ½ tsp butterscotch flavouring 1 pinch salt condensed milk	Combine the flour and the baking powder and sift into a mixing bowl. Add the quark, milk, oil, sugar, vanilla sugar, butterscotch flavouring and salt. Use the dough hook of a hand mixer to work the mixture into a dough at full speed for about 1 minute (not too long or the dough will be sticky). Then shape the dough into a roll on the floured work surface. Roll out the dough into a rectangle measuring about 40 x 35 cm (16 x 14 inch). Spread the filling on top, leaving about 1 cm (½ inch) free at the edges. Brush the edges with condensed milk. Roll up the dough, starting from the longest side. Using a sharp knife, make a single lengthways incision. Take care to divide the roll exactly in the middle, so that the plait will rise evenly. Wind the two strands of dough around one another, with the dough side towards the bottom. Place the plait on a greased baking sheet and press the ends firmly together.

Oven temperatures	
Conventional oven	about 170°C/325°F (preheated)
Fan-assisted oven	140–150°C/275–300°F (not preheated)
Gas oven	about mark 3 (preheated)
Baking time	about 45 minutes (cover the plait after 25 minutes, if necessary).

For the apricot glaze

3 tbsp apricot jam 2 tbsp water	Press the apricot jam through a sieve and bring briefly to the boil with the water, stirring continuously. Glaze the plait immediately after baking.

Preparation required

Bake choux paste on a lightly greased baking sheet dusted with flour.
Sift a small quantity of flour on to one side of the baking sheet. To ensure that the flour is evenly distributed and does not form too thick a layer, tap the unfloured side of the baking sheet gently against the work surface to dislodge the excess flour.

Sift the flour and the cornflour.
Mixing and sifting the flour (with the exception of wholemeal flour) and cornflour breaks up the particles and ensures that they are evenly distributed. For the next step, it is a good idea to sift the dry ingredients on to a sheet of non-stick baking paper.
If you are using wholemeal flour, measure it out beforehand and place on one side ready for use.

The individual steps

Bring the water and fat to the boil, preferably in a long-handled heavy-based saucepan. Remove the pan from the heat and add the sifted dry ingredients (flour and cornflour) all at once.
It is important for the flour and cornflour mixture not to form lumps. For this reason, remove the pan of boiling water and fat from the heat and add all the sifted flour and cornflour at once. Never sprinkle it in gradually.

Stir to form a smooth ball...
As soon as the flour and cornflour have been added to the hot water, stir vigorously until a smooth ball of paste is formed.

...and heat the paste, still stirring, for a further 1 minute.
This makes the paste firmer. A thin skin on the bottom of the pan indicates that the paste has been heated for a sufficient length of time. You will need to use quite a high heat.

Immediately place the hot ball of paste in a bowl.
Further beating of the paste should be with a dough hook. It is advisable to place the ball of paste in a bowl.

Gradually work in the eggs at full speed.
Add the eggs to the hot paste. First break each egg into a cup to check for freshness. Add the eggs to the paste gradually, as this makes it easier for them to be thoroughly incorporated.

Stop adding eggs when the paste is very shiny and slips off a spoon leaving long strands behind.
Since eggs vary in size, test the paste after adding the second-last egg. If the paste is already very shiny and slips off a spoon leaving long strands behind, do not add any more eggs; if the paste is too soft, the finished dough will not hold its shape. Otherwise, beat the last egg but add only as much as necessary.

Then add the baking powder to the cooled paste.
Baking powder must never be brought into direct contact with warm ingredients before baking, since it would start to work too early and would not raise the dough during baking. This is why when making choux paste, the baking powder is not mixed with the flour but is added at the end.

If the paste is to be used for cream puffs, for example, use two teaspoons to place heaps of the paste on a prepared baking sheet, or pipe it on with a piping bag. If the paste is to be fried, use two teaspoons to drop small amounts into the pan. Alternatively, small circles may be piped on to greased pieces of non-stick baking paper, which are then dropped into the hot fat or oil.

Baking choux paste

All types of choux paste are baked as specified in the recipes. Only towards the end of the baking time may the oven door be carefully opened to check progress. If the oven door is opened earlier, the paste will collapse.

The finished product should be light and airy. The inner cavity should no longer be moist. If the paste is to be fried, the fat or oil should first be brought to a sufficiently high temperature, so that the paste does not absorb too much of it and become soggy.

Basic recipe
Grundrezept

125 ml (4 fl oz) water **25 g (1 oz) margarine or butter** **75 g (3 oz) plain flour** **1 tbsp cornflour**	Bring the water and margarine or butter to the boil, preferably in a long-handled pan. Mix together the flour and the cornflour and sieve. Remove the pan from the heat and empty all the flour mixture into the liquid. Stir to form a smooth ball and heat for one minute, stirring continuously.
2-3 eggs	Immediately place the warm ball of paste in a bowl and gradually work in the eggs at full speed, using the dough hook of a hand mixer. The amount of egg to be added depends on the appearance of the dough. It must be very shiny and slide off a spoon leaving long strands behind.
1 pinch baking powder	Work the baking powder into the cooled paste. Process and bake as specified in the recipe.

Cherry Puff
for guests

Flockentorte (see photo on pages 184/185)

For the shortcrust base

150 g (5½ oz) plain flour **40 g (1½ oz) sugar** **2 tsp vanilla sugar** **100 g (3½ oz) margarine or butter**	Sift the flour into a mixing bowl and add the sugar, vanilla sugar and margarine or butter. Use the dough hook of a hand mixer to process the ingredients thoroughly, first at low speed and then at full speed. Then knead the mixture on the work surface to form a smooth dough. Chill the dough for a while if it is sticky. Roll out the dough on the greased base of a 28 cm (11 inch) springform tin and prick it in several times with a fork. Fit the rim of the springform tin around the base.
Oven temperatures	
Conventional oven	200–220°C/400–425°F (preheated)
Fan-assisted oven	170–180°C /350–375°F (not preheated)
Gas oven	mark 3–4 (preheated)
Baking time	about 15 minutes.

Loosen the shortcrust from the springform base immediately after baking. Allow to cool on the base and then transfer to a cake dish.

For the choux paste

125 ml (4 fl oz) water **25 g (1 oz) margarine or butter** **75 g (3 oz) plain flour** **1 tbsp cornflour**	Bring the water and margarine or butter to the boil, preferably in a long-handled saucepan. Combine the flour and the cornflour and sift them. Remove the pan from the heat and empty all the flour mixture into the liquid. Stir to form a smooth ball and cook for one minute, stirring constantly.

2-3 eggs
1 pinch baking powder

Immediately place the warm ball of paste in a bowl and gradually work in the eggs at full speed, using the dough hook of a hand mixer. The amount of egg to be added depends on the appearance of the dough. It must be very shiny and slide off a spoon leaving long strands behind.
Work the baking powder into the cooled paste.
Bake three paste bases, in each case spreading a third of the paste over the greased and floured base of a 28 cm (11 inch) springform tin. Make sure that the paste is not too thin at the edges, so that it does not become too dark.
Bake each paste base, without the rim of the springform tin in position, until light brown.

Oven temperatures	
Conventional oven	200–220°C/400–425°F (preheated)
Fan-assisted oven	170–180°C /350–375°F (not preheated)
Gas oven	mark 4–5 (preheated)
Baking time	20–25 minutes.

Loosen the pastry bases from the tin immediately after baking and leave to cool individually on a wire rack (this is important, as the steam needs to evaporate).

For the filling

500 g (18 oz) canned cherries, stoned with juice
2 tbsp cornflour

Drain the cherries, reserving the juice. Measure out 250 ml (9 fl oz) of the juice (top up with water if necessary).
Stir the cornflour into 4 tablespoons of the juice. Bring the rest of the juice to the boil and remove the pan from the heat. Stir in the cornflour mixture and bring briefly to the boil once again. Stir in the cherries and leave to cool. Add sugar to taste.

sugar
500 ml (18 fl oz) double cream
25 g (1 oz) icing sugar
2 tsp vanilla sugar
15 g (1 tbsp) cream of tartar

Whip the cream for 30 seconds. Sift the icing sugar, mix with the vanilla sugar and cream of tartar and sprinkle over the cream. Whip the cream until stiff.

redcurrant jelly

Spread a thin layer of redcurrant jelly over the shortcrust base and place a layer of choux paste on top. Spread this with half the cherry mixture and then about a third of the cream. Cover with the second layer of choux paste and spread this with the rest of the cherry mixture and the cream. Break the third layer of choux paste into pieces and arrange on top of the cream.

2 tbsp icing sugar

Dust with icing sugar.

Eclairs

easy

Eclairs oder Liebesknochen

For the paste

125 ml (4 fl oz) water **25 g (1 oz) margarine or butter** **75 g (3 oz) plain flour** **1 tbsp cornflour**	Bring the water and margarine or butter to the boil, preferably in a long-handled saucepan. Combine the flour and the cornflour and sift them. Remove the pan from the heat and empty all the flour mixture into the liquid. Stir to form a smooth ball and cook for one minute, stirring continuously.
2-3 eggs	Immediately place the warm ball of paste in a bowl and gradually work in the eggs at full speed, using the dough hook of a hand mixer. The amount of egg to be added depends on the appearance of the dough. It should be very shiny and slide off a spoon leaving long strands behind.
1 pinch baking powder	Work the baking powder into the cooled paste. Place in a piping bag and, using a large star nozzle, pipe 6 cm (2½ inch) lengths on to a greased baking sheet dusted with flour. Another option is to pipe two finger-length strips next to one another and then add a third on top.

Oven temperatures	
Conventional oven	200–220°C/400–425°F (preheated)
Fan-assisted oven	170–180°C /350–375°F (not preheated)
Gas oven	mark 4–5 (preheated)
Baking time	about 20 minutes.

Cut off a 'lid' from each eclair immediately after baking and leave to cool.

For the apricot glaze

apricot jam	Press the apricot jam through a sieve and heat, stirring continuously. Brush a thin layer of glaze over the lids of the eclairs.

For the filling

75 g (3 oz) chocolate nut spread	Heat the chocolate nut spread in a small pan over a bain-marie, stirring until smooth. Leave to cool slightly.
250 ml (9 fl oz) double cream **2 tsp cream of tartar**	Whip the cream for 30 seconds. Sprinkle with the cream of tartar and whip until stiff. Carefully stir in the chocolate spread, a tablespoon at a time. Put the chocolate cream in a piping bag and, using a star nozzle, pipe the filling into the eclairs. Place a lid on top of each eclair.

Variation **Eclairs with chocolate cream and strawberries**

For the filling

300 g (10½ oz) milk chocolate 400 ml (14 fl oz) double cream	Break the chocolate into pieces. Bring the cream to the boil and remove the pan from the heat. Stir in the chocolate and keep stirring until it has completely dissolved. Leave to cool for at least 2 hours.
400 g (14 oz) strawberries	Wash, wipe and thinly slice the strawberries. Use the whisk of a hand mixer to whisk the chocolate cream for about 10 minutes, until it is smooth. Cut the eclairs in half lengthways. Put the chocolate cream in a piping bag and pipe it on to the bases. Top with the strawberries.
40 g (1½ oz) white chocolate cake covering	Melt the white chocolate covering in a small pan over a bain-marie and use a teaspoon to trace thin lines over the top of the eclairs.

Variation **Fruit eclairs**

For the filling

1 tsp unflavoured gelatine 1 tbsp water 2 tsp sugar grated rind of untread orange 250 ml (9 fl oz) double cream	Prepare the gelatine according to the package directions with water and sugar. Whip the cream until almost stiff. Gradually add the orange-flavoured jelly and whip until completely stiff. Spread a little of the orange cream on the underside of each lid. Spoon the rest of the cream into the eclairs and place the lids on top, cream side up.
about 200 g (7 oz) canned mandarin segments	Drain the mandarin segments and arrange decoratively on the lids.

Cream Puffs

Windbeutel

quick

For the paste

125 ml (4 fl oz) water 25 g (1 oz) margarine or butter 75 g (3 oz) plain flour 1 tbsp cornflour	Bring the water and margarine or butter to the boil, preferably in a long-handled saucepan. Combine the flour and the cornflour and sift them. Remove the pan from the heat and empty all the flour mixture into the liquid. Stir to form a smooth ball and heat for one minute, stirring continuously.
2-3 eggs	Immediately place the warm ball of paste in a bowl and gradually work in the eggs at full speed, using the dough hook of a hand mixer. The amount of egg to be added depends on the appearance of the dough. It must be very shiny and slide off a spoon leaving long strands behind.
1 pinch baking powder	Work the baking powder into the cooled paste. Use two spoons or a piping bag to place eight heaps of paste on a greased baking sheet dusted with flour.

Oven temperatures	
Conventional oven	200–220°C/400–425°F (preheated)
Fan-assisted oven	170–180°C/350°F (not preheated)
Gas oven	mark 4–5 (preheated)
Baking time	25–30 minutes.

Do not open the oven door during the first 15 minutes of baking, or the choux paste will collapse. Immediately after baking, cut off a lid from each cream puff and leave to cool.

For the filling

250 g (9 oz) redcurrants 30 g (1 oz) icing sugar 125 g (4½ oz) low-fat soft cheese 2 tbsp red- or blackcurrant liqueur 1 tsp lemon juice 250 ml (9 fl oz) double cream 2 tsp vanilla sugar 2 tsp cream of tartar 50 g (2 oz) blanched, slivered almonds 4 tsp icing sugar	Dust the redcurrants with the icing sugar. Mix together the low fat soft cheese, liqueur and lemon juice. Whip the cream and vanilla sugar until stiff and fold in the quark mixture and redcurrants. Lightly toast the slivered almonds in a dry frying pan and leave to cool. Fold into the mixture. Divide the filling between the cream puffs and replace the lids. Dust with icing sugar.

Cheese Puffs

Käsewindbeutelchen

for guests

For the choux paste

125 ml (4 fl oz) water 1 pinch salt 25 g (1 oz) margarine or butter 75 g (3 oz) plain flour 1 tbsp cornflour 2-3 eggs	Bring the water, salt and margarine or butter to the boil, preferably in a long-handled heavy-based saucepan. Mix together the flour and the cornflour and sift them. Remove the pan from the heat and empty all the flour mixture into the liquid. Stir to form a smooth ball and heat for one minute, stirring continuously. Immediately place the warm ball of paste in a bowl and gradually work in the eggs at full speed, using the dough hook of a hand mixer. The amount of egg to be added depends on the appearance of the dough. It must be very shiny and slide off a spoon leaving long strands behind.
½ tsp baking powder 100 g (3 ½ oz) grated Emmental cheese	Work the baking powder into the cooled paste. Finally, fold in the grated cheese.
plain flour	Use two teaspoons to arrange walnut-sized heaps of paste on a greased baking sheet dusted with flour.
Oven temperatures	
Conventional oven	200–220°C/400–425°F (preheated)
Fan-assisted oven	170–180°C/350°F (not preheated)
Gas oven	mark 4–5 (preheated)
Baking time	about 20 minutes.

Immediately after baking, cut off a lid from each paste puff. Leave to cool.

For the filling

200 g (7 oz) double cream cheese (such as mascarpone) 150 ml (5 fl oz) crème fraîche salt freshly-ground black pepper 100 g (3 ½ oz) smoked ham paprika	Combine the cream cheese and crème fraîche. Season to taste with salt and freshly ground pepper. Dice the ham and stir it into the mixture. Fill the choux puffs and replace the lids. Dust them with paprika.

Preparation

Strudel dough is for people who only want a little crispy pastry but plenty of filling. Using the right technique when pulling the dough over the back of your hand (not as difficult as is often assumed), you can prepare this delicious pastry.

To prepare the dough, weigh the ingredients carefully and thoroughly grease the baking sheet or Swiss roll tin.

The dough needs a fairly warm environment for proving. In order to create it, boil some water in a saucepan so that the saucepan takes on the heat. Then pour out the water and leave the saucepan to dry.

Method

Sift the flour into a mixing bowl (except if using wholemeal flour) and make a well in the centre.

Put salt, egg (if using), water and fat in the well.

Process the ingredients using the kneading attachment on a blender or food mixer, first briefly on the lowest setting, then for longer on the highest setting.

The dough should be elastic, but not too soft or sticky. If this is the case, add a little more flour.

Once the dough has been kneaded thoroughly, shape it into a ball.
Then place the dough on non-stick baking paper into the hot, dry saucepan; put the lid on the saucepan and leave the dough to prove for about 30 minutes.

Roll out the dough on a large, floured tea towel and brush lightly with a little melted fat.

Using the back of your hand, pull the dough into a rectangle about 50 x 70 cm (20 x 28 inches) until it is transparent (the pattern of the tea towel should be visible through the dough). Continue to brush the strudel with fat, both before and during baking. This will make it more moist.
Cut off the thick edges.
Continue as described in the recipe.

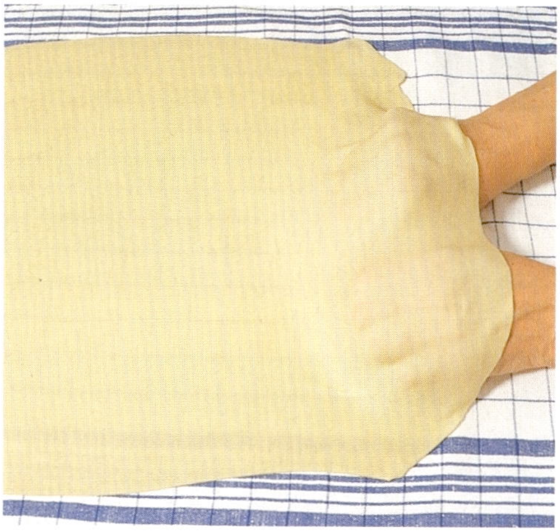

Basic recipe
Grundrezept

For strudel dough with egg

250 g (9 oz) strong plain flour
1 pinch salt
100 ml (3 ½ fl oz) lukewarm water
1 small egg
1 tbsp vegetable oil

Sift the flour into a mixing bowl and add the salt, water, egg and oil.

or,

for strudel dough without egg

200 g (7 oz) strong plain flour
1 pinch salt
75 ml (2½ fl oz) lukewarm water
50 ml (2 fl oz) vegetable oil

Sift the flour into a mixing bowl and add the salt, water and oil. Mix the ingredients using the kneading attachment of a hand-held blender or food mixer, at first briefly on the lowest setting, then longer on the highest setting. Then knead on the work surface to make a smooth dough.

Place the dough on non-stick baking paper in a hot, dry saucepan (boil some water in it first); put the lid on the saucepan and leave the dough to prove for about 30 minutes.

50 g (2 oz) melted margarine or butter or vegetable oil

Roll out the dough on a large floured tea towel or a tablecloth. Brush it lightly with a little of the fat. Lift up the dough and pull it out over the back of your hand to form a 50 x 70 cm (20 x 28 inch) rectangle. The dough should be transparent. If the edges are a little thicker, trim them. Brush the dough with a little fat. The rest of the ingredients and the method depend upon the recipe.

Viennese Apple Strudel

popular

Wiener Apfelstrudel (see photograph on pages 196/197)

	For the dough
200 g (7 oz) strong plain flour **1 pinch salt** **75 ml (2 ½ fl oz) lukewarm water** **50 g (2 oz) melted margarine or butter or 3 tbsp vegetable oil**	Sift the flour into a mixing bowl and add the salt, water and fat. Process the ingredients using a hand-held blender with a kneading attachment: at first briefly on the lowest setting, then thoroughly on the highest setting; then knead the dough on the work surface until smooth.
	Place the dough on non-stick baking paper in a hot, dry saucepan (boil some water in it first); put the lid on the saucepan and leave the dough to prove for about 30 minutes.
	For the filling
1–1½ kg (2 lb 4 oz-3 lb) apples **¼ tsp rum essence** **3 drops lemon essence** **75 g (3 oz) margarine or butter**	Peel, quarter and core the apples and cut into thin slices. Add the rum and lemon essences. Melt the margarine or butter.
	Roll out the dough on a large floured tea towel or tablecloth. Brush the dough thinly with a little of the fat; then pull it with your hands to form a 50 x 70 cm (20 x 28 inch) rectangle. The dough should be transparent. If the edges are a little thicker, cut them off.
50 g (2 oz) biscuit or cake crumbs **50 g (2 oz) raisins** **100 g (3 ½ oz) sugar** **2 tsp vanilla sugar** **50 g (2 oz) blanched, chopped almonds**	Brush two-thirds of the fat over the dough. Scatter the cake or biscuit crumbs over two-thirds of the dough, leaving about 3 cm (1 inch) bare at the shorter ends. Then, in order of the ingredients, arrange the apples, raisins, sugar, vanilla sugar and blanched, chopped almonds on the dough. Fold the free edges of the dough over the filling. Then, use the tea towel to help roll up the dough from the longer edge, starting with the filling. Press down well at the ends, place on a greased baking sheet and brush with a little fat.
Oven temperatures	
Conventional oven	170–200°C/350–400°F (preheated)
Fan-assisted oven	160–170°C/325–350°F (not preheated)
Gas oven	mark 3–4 (preheated)
Baking time	45–55 minutes.
	After 30 minutes, brush the strudel with the remaining fat.
Tip	Bake two small strudels instead of one large one.

East German Poppyseed Strudel

traditional

Ostdeutscher Mohnstrudel

For the dough

- 250 g (9 oz) strong plain flour
- 1 pinch salt
- 75 ml (3 fl oz) lukewarm water
- 50 ml (2 fl oz) vegetable oil

Sift the flour into a mixing bowl and add the salt, water and oil. Mix the ingredients using the kneading attachment of a hand-held blender or food mixer, at first briefly on the lowest setting, then longer on the highest setting. Then knead on the work surface to make a smooth dough.

Place the dough on non-stick baking paper in a hot, dry saucepan (boil some water in it first); put the lid on the saucepan and leave the dough to prove for about 30 minutes.

For the filling

- 300 g (10½ oz) freshly ground poppyseeds
- 300 ml (10 fl oz) boiling milk
- 75 g (3 oz) sugar
- 2 tbsp honey
- 1 egg
- 1 tsp finely chopped candied lemon peel
- 100 g (3½ oz) raisins
- 250 g (9 oz) cooking apples

Pour the boiling milk over the poppyseeds (photo 1) and stir. Leave to soak until soft. Mix in the sugar, honey, egg, candied peel and raisins. Peel, core and coarsely grate the apples and stir into the poppyseed mixture.

- 50 g (2 oz) melted butter

Roll out the dough on a large floured cloth (tea towel) to form a 50 x 40 cm (20 x 16 inch) rectangle. Spread the filling on 2/3 of the dough, leaving about 3 cm at the shorter ends (photo 2). Then, using the tea towel, roll up the dough, starting with the filling. Press down well at the ends (photo 3), place on a greased baking sheet and brush with some of the butter. While the strudel is baking, brush with the remaining butter.

(continued on page 204)

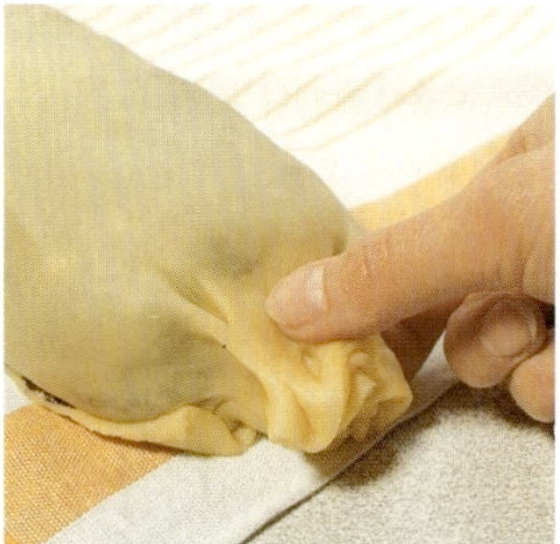

Oven temperatures	
Conventional oven	180–200°C/350–400°F (preheated)
Fan-assisted oven	160–180°C/325–350°F (not preheated)
Gas oven	mark 3–4 (preheated)
Baking time	about 50 minutes.

icing sugar — Dust the strudel with icing sugar.

Tip — Sprinkle the strudel with flaked almonds before baking.

Serving suggestion — Serve with custard.

Quark Strudel

Topfenstrudel (Quarkstrudel)

traditional

125 g (4½ oz) strong plain flour
1 pinch salt
1 egg
2 tbsp lukewarm water
2 tbsp vegetable oil

For the dough

Sift the flour into a mixing bowl and add the salt, egg, water and oil. Mix the ingredients using the kneading attachment of a hand-held blender or food mixer, at first briefly on the lowest setting, then longer on the highest setting. Then knead on the work surface to make a smooth dough.
Place the dough on non-stick baking paper in a hot, dry saucepan (boil some water in it first); put the lid on the saucepan and leave the dough to prove for about 30 minutes.

40 g (1½ oz) margarine or butter
40 g (1½ oz) sugar
1 egg
1 tbsp lemon juice
180 g (6½ oz) low-fat soft cheese
1 packet custard powder
2 tbsp double cream

For the filling

Cream the margarine or butter, gradually adding the sugar, egg, lemon juice, low-fat soft cheese, custard powder and cream.

40 g (1½ oz) softened butter **50 g (2 oz) raisins**	Roll out the dough on a large floured cloth to form a 50 x 40 cm (20 x 16 inch) rectangle. The dough should be transparent. Trim off the thicker edges. Brush the dough with some of the butter and spread the filling over two-thirds of the dough, leaving about 3 cm (1 inch) bare at the sides. Sprinkle with the raisins.
420 g (15 oz) canned apricots	Thoroughly drain the apricots, cut them into small pieces and sprinkle them over the cheese. Fold the free ends over the filling. Then, use the tea towel to help roll up the dough, starting with the filling. Press down well at the ends and place on a greased baking sheet. Brush with more butter.
Oven temperatures	
Conventional oven	170–200°C/350–400°F (preheated)
Fan-assisted oven	160–170°C/325–350°F (not preheated)
Gas oven	mark 3–4 (preheated)
Baking time	40–50 minutes.
sifted icing sugar	After 30 minutes, brush the strudel with the remaining butter. Leave the strudel to cool down. If desired, dust with icing sugar.
Tip	Serve with custard.
Variation	**Quark strudel with dried fruit**
125 g (4½ oz) mixed dried fruit **1 egg yolk** **35 g (1¼ oz) sugar** **2 tbsp vanilla sugar** **1-2 tbsp lemon juice** **200 g (7 oz) double-cream cheese (such as mascarpone)** **125 g (4½ oz) low-fat soft cheese** **2 egg whites** **25 g (1 oz) chopped pine kernels** **1 egg yolk mixed**	**For the filling** Dice the dried fruit. Blend the egg yolk with the sugar, vanilla sugar and lemon juice until very creamy. Mix in the double-cream cheese with the low-fat cheese. Whisk the egg whites until very stiff and fold into the cheese mixture. Spread the filling onto the dough and sprinkle with the fruit and pine kernels. Roll up the strudel as above and brush with beaten egg yolk before baking.

Cherry pastries

Kirschbeutelchen

for children

For the dough

250 g (9 oz) strong plain flour
1 pinch salt
100 ml (3½ fl oz) lukewarm water
1 small egg
1 tbsp vegetable oil

Sift the flour into a mixing bowl and add the salt, water, egg and oil. Process the ingredients using a hand-held blender with a kneading attachment: at first briefly on the lowest setting, then thoroughly on the highest setting; then knead on the work surface to make a smooth dough. Place the dough on non-stick baking paper in a hot, dry saucepan (boil some water in it first); put the lid on the saucepan and leave the dough to prove for about 30 minutes.

For the filling

60 g (2½ oz) margarine or butter
2 egg yolks
100 g (3½ oz) marzipan
350 g (12 oz) canned sour cherries
30 g (1 oz) sponge fingers
50 g (2 oz) blanched, ground almonds

Melt the margarine or butter and leave to cool. Stir in the egg yolks. Dice the marzipan. Drain the morello cherries in a sieve. Crush the biscuits and prepare the almonds.

Roll out the dough on a large floured cloth to form a 50 x 40 cm (20 x 16 inch) rectangle. The dough should be transparent. Trim off the thicker edges. Cut the dough into 12 x 12 cm (4½ x 4½ inch) squares, brush with the butter/egg mixture, sprinkle with the biscuit crumbs and almonds and place the cherries and marzipan on top (4-5 cherries per square).

50 g (2 oz) melted butter

Fold the dough over the filling to make small pockets, place on a greased baking sheet and brush with some of the melted butter.

Oven temperatures

Conventional oven	170–200°C/350–400°F (preheated)
Fan-assisted oven	160–170°C/325–350°F (not preheated)
Gas oven	mark 3–4 (preheated)
Baking time	about 10 minutes.

icing sugar

Brush the pastries with the remaining butter during baking. Serve hot or cold, dusting with icing sugar before serving.

Serving suggestion Serve with thick custard.

For the yeast dough

Sift the flour into a mixing bowl (unless you are using wholemeal flour) and thoroughly stir in the Easyblend yeast with a fork. Add the rest of the dry ingredients (sugar, vanilla sugar, salt.)

Add all the remaining ingredients listed in the recipe (crème fraîche, milk, egg) to the flour. Yeast can only develop its full rising action in a warm environment - the liquid (milk) especially should be hand-hot (37°C/98.6°F). Process the ingredients using the kneading attachment on a hand-held blender or food processor. Knead briefly on the lowest setting, then for about 5 minutes on the highest setting. The dough must be smooth.

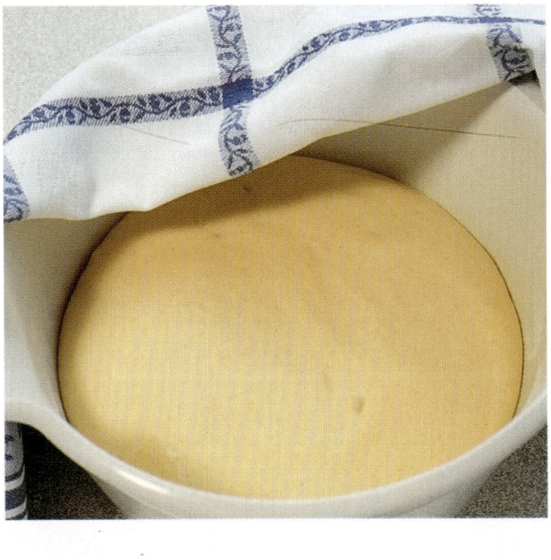

Cover the dough with a tea towel or with clingfilm and leave to prove in a warm place until it has visibly risen.
Don't bake the yeast dough immediately after preparing it but leave to prove sufficiently. Put it in a warm place, such as a gas or electric oven, with the heat turned off.
Gas: Preheat on mark 8 for 3 minutes **then turn off the gas.**
Electric: Set to 50°C/112°F and place the bowl containing the dough in the oven until the dough has visibly risen. Wedge the oven door open with a wooden spoon.
Microwave: 80 or 90 watts for about 8 minutes. If the microwave doesn't have a turntable, turn the bowl around after about 4 minutes.
Bain-marie: Place the bowl with the dough, covered with a damp cloth, in hot water until the dough has visibly risen.
Also see pages 94-95 for working with yeast dough.

For the shortcrust dough

Sift the flour into a mixing bowl and add the fat.
Sifting loosens the grains of flour, but do not sift if you are using wholemeal flour.

Process the ingredients using a hand-held blender with a kneading attachment, first briefly on the lowest setting, then thoroughly on the highest setting.
Then knead by hand on a work surface to make a smooth dough. The ingredients will combine best if the fat is softened (spreadable) so remove it from the refrigerator in good time.

For the combined dough

Then, on a floured work surface, knead both doughs together by hand until smooth.
Do not put too much flour on the work surface, otherwise the dough may break up. Pummel the dough quickly with both hands with the flat of your knuckles. Then follow the recipe instructions for the rest of the preparation and baking.

Basic recipe

Grundrezept

For the yeast dough

- 250 g (9 oz) strong plain flour
- 1 sachet Easyblend yeast
- 25 g (1 oz) sugar
- 2 tsp vanilla sugar
- 1 pinch salt
- 1 egg
- 125 ml (9 fl oz) lukewarm milk
- or
- 150 ml (5 fl oz) crème fraîche

Thoroughly mix the flour and yeast. Add the sugar, vanilla sugar, salt, egg and the milk or crème fraîche. Process the ingredients using a hand-held blender with a kneading attachment: first briefly on the lowest setting, then for approximately 5 minutes on the highest setting to form a dough.

Cover the dough and leave to prove in a warm place until it has visibly risen.

For the shortcrust dough

- 100 g (3½ oz) plain flour
- 25 g (1 oz) sugar
- 2 tsp vanilla sugar
- 1 pinch salt
- 50 g (2 oz) margarine or butter

Sift the flour into a mixing bowl. Add the sugar, vanilla sugar, salt and the margarine or butter. Process the ingredients using the kneading attachment on a hand-held blender or food processor, first briefly on the lowest setting, then thoroughly on the highest setting. Then knead on a work surface to form a smooth dough.

Lightly dust the risen yeast dough with flour, remove from the bowl and, on the work surface, thoroughly knead it into the short-crust dough. Depending on the recipe, leave the dough to prove again in the baking tin or baking sheet. Bake as instructed in the recipe.

Basic savoury recipe

Grundrezept pikant

For the yeast dough

200 g (7 oz) strong plain flour
1 sachet Easyblend yeast
1 tsp salt
100 ml (3½ fl oz) lukewarm milk
50 g (2 oz) melted and cooled margarine or butter

Sieve the flour into a mixing bowl and thoroughly mix in the yeast. Add the salt, milk and melted, cooled margarine or butter. Process the ingredients using a hand-held blender with a kneading attachment, first briefly on the lowest setting, then for approximately 5 minutes on the highest setting to form a dough. Cover the dough and leave to prove in a warm place until it has visibly risen.

For the shortcrust dough

100 g (3½ oz) plain flour
1 pinch baking powder
1 pinch salt
75 g (3 oz) margarine or butter

Mix the flour and baking powder and sieve into a mixing bowl. Add the salt and the margarine or butter. Process the ingredients using a hand-held blender with a kneading attachment, first briefly on the lowest setting, then for approximately 5 minutes on the highest setting. Then knead on a work surface to form a smooth dough.

Lightly dust the risen yeast dough with flour, remove from the bowl and thoroughly knead into the shortcrust dough on a work surface. Arrange the dough in a baking tin or baking sheet, depending on the recipe. Bake as per the recipe.

Vanilla and cherry cake

for guests

Vanille-Kirsch-Kuchen (see photo on pages 208/209)

For the yeast dough

- 250 g (9 oz) strong plain flour
- 1 sachet Easyblend yeast
- 25 g (1 oz) sugar
- 2 tsp vanilla sugar
- 1 pinch salt
- 1 egg
- 150 ml (5 fl oz) crème fraîche

Sieve the flour into a mixing bowl and thoroughly mix in the yeast. Add the sugar, vanilla sugar, salt, egg and crème fraîche. Process the ingredients using a hand-held blender with a kneading attachment: first briefly on the lowest setting, then for approximately 5 minutes on the highest setting to form a dough. Cover the dough and leave to prove in a warm place until it has visibly risen.

For the shortcrust dough

- 100 g (3½ oz) plain flour
- 25 g (1 oz) sugar
- 2 tsp vanilla sugar
- 1 pinch salt
- 1 egg
- 50 g (2 oz) margarine or butter

Sift the flour into a mixing bowl. Add the sugar, vanilla sugar, salt, egg and the margarine or butter. Process the ingredients using a hand-held blender with a kneading attachment, first briefly on the lowest setting, then thoroughly on the highest setting. Then knead on a work surface to form a smooth dough.

For the filling

- 2 packets vanilla pudding powder
- 50 g (2 oz) sugar
- 2 egg yolks
- 750 ml (1¼ pints) milk
- 3 egg whites
- 500 ml (18 fl oz) double cream

Following the packet instructions, make the vanilla pudding, using the sugar and egg yolks but only 750 ml (1¼ pints) milk. Whisk the egg whites until stiff and stir at once into the boiling hot blancmange; leave to cool down a little. Stir in the double cream and leave the blancmange to cool down.

Lightly dust the risen yeast dough with flour. Place it on the work surface and thoroughly knead it into the shortcrust dough. Roll out half of the dough on a 38 x 28 cm (15 x 11 inch) greased baking sheet and spread the cooled pudding on the dough.

- 700 g (1lb 9 oz) canned sour cherries
- 1 egg yolk
- 1 tbsp condensed milk
- sugar mixed with ground cinnamon
- 50 g (2 oz) blanched, slivered almonds

Thoroughly drain the cherries and place them on top of the pudding. Roll out the remaining dough to the same size as the baking sheet, place it on top of the cherries and press down at the edges. Beat the egg yolk with the condensed milk and brush over the dough. Sprinkle with the sugar-and-cinnamon mixture and the almonds. Once again leave the dough to prove in a warm place until it has risen visibly.

Oven temperatures	
Conventional oven	170–200°C/400°F (preheated)
Fan-assisted oven	160–170°C/350°F (not preheated)
Gas oven	mark 3–4 (preheated)
Baking time	about 30 minutes.

Hazelnut bread

Haselnußbrot

For the combined dough

125 ml (4 fl oz) milk

Follow the basic recipe on page 212 and adding the milk, prepare a combined dough.

For the filling

100 g (3½ oz) ground hazelnuts
100 g (3½ oz) coarsely chopped hazelnuts
50 g (2 oz) sugar
¼ tsp butterscotch flavouring
1 egg
3-4 tbsp water

Stir together the hazelnuts, sugar, butterscotch flavouring, egg and water to form a smooth mixture.

On a work surface, thoroughly knead together the risen yeast dough with the shortcrust dough. Roll it out to form a 30 x 45 cm (12 x 18 inch) rectangle. Spread the filling over it and, starting from the narrow edge, roll up the dough towards the middle. Then roll towards the middle from the other side, place in a greased, floured 30 x 11 cm (12 x 4 inch) baking tin and leave to prove in a warm place once more until the dough has visibly risen.

condensed milk

Brush with condensed milk.

Oven temperatures	
Conventional oven	170–200°C/400°F (preheated)
Fan-assisted oven	160–170°C/350°F (not preheated)
Gas oven	mark 3–4 (not preheated)
Baking time	35–40 minutes.

Apricot rosette cake

Aprikosen-Rosetten-Kuchen

sophisticated

For the filling

125 g (4½ oz) dried apricots
5 tbsp rum
1 packet vanilla pudding powder
375 ml (13 fl oz) milk
2 tsp vanilla sugar
125 ml (4 fl oz) double cream

Finely dice the dried apricots, stir in the rum and ideally leave to soak overnight. Following the packet instructions, make the pudding using only 375 ml (13 fl oz) milk. Leave to cool down a little. Stir in the vanilla sugar, double cream and the soaked apricots. Leave to cool, stirring occasionally.

For the yeast dough

275 g (9½ oz) strong plain flour
1 sachet Easyblend dry yeast
75 g (3 oz) sugar
2 tsp vanilla sugar
¼ tsp lemon essence
1 pinch salt
1 egg
150 ml (5 fl oz) crème fraîche
4 tbsp lukewarm milk

Sift the flour into a mixing bowl and thoroughly mix in the yeast. Add the sugar, vanilla sugar, lemon essence, salt, egg, crème fraîche and milk. Process the ingredients using a hand-held blender with a kneading attachment, first briefly on the lowest setting, then for approximately 5 minutes on the highest setting. When the dough is smooth and kneaded, cover it and leave to prove in a warm place until it has visibly risen.

For the shortcrust dough

100 g (3½ oz) strong plain flour
30 g (1 oz) sugar
2 tsp vanilla sugar
1 pinch salt
60 g (2¼ oz) margarine or butter

Sift the flour into a mixing bowl. Add the sugar, vanilla sugar, salt and the margarine or butter. Process the ingredients using a hand-held blender with a kneading attachment, first briefly on the lowest setting, then for approximately 5 minutes on the highest setting. Then knead on a work surface to form a smooth dough.

Lightly dust the risen yeast dough with flour, remove from the bowl and, on the work surface, thoroughly knead into the shortcrust pastry. Roll out to form a 50 x 30 cm (20 x 12 inch) rectangle and spread the filling over the dough, leaving a 1 cm (½ inch) edge. Roll up the dough from the longer edge, cut into pieces 3 cm (1 inch) wide. Grease the base of a 28 cm (11 inch) diameter springform tin. Place the pieces side by side and leave to prove in a warm place until it has risen visibly.

(continued on page 218)

Oven temperatures	
Conventional oven	170–200°C/350–400°F (preheated)
Fan-assisted oven	160–170°C/335–350°F (not preheated)
Gas oven	mark 3–4 (preheated)
Baking time	about 45 minutes.
	Remove the cake from the tin.

To glaze

2 tbsp apricot jam
2 tbsp water
ground pistachio nuts

Rub the apricot jam through a sieve. Bring to the boil with the water and, stirring, reduce a little. Brush the cake with the glaze immediately after baking. If desired, sprinkle with ground pistachio nuts.

Apple spelt cakes

Apfel-Jalousien

For the yeast dough

250 g (9 oz) spelt flour
1 sachet Easyblend dry yeast
40 g (1½ oz) honey
2 tsp muscovado sugar
1 tsp rum essence
1 pinch salt
1 egg
pinch of ground cinnamon
100 ml (3½ fl oz) lukewarm milk

Put the flour and yeast into a mixing bowl and thoroughly mix in the honey. Add the muscovado sugar, rum essence, salt, egg, cinnamon and milk. Process the ingredients using a hand-held blender with a kneading attachment, at first briefly on the lowest setting, then for approximately 5 minutes on the highest setting, to make a dough.
Cover the dough and leave to prove in a warm place until it has visibly risen.

For the shortcrust dough

100 g (3½ oz) spelt flour
40 g (1½ oz) demerara sugar
2 tsp muscovado sugar
1 egg
50 g (2 oz) butter

Put the flour into a mixing bowl. Add the demerara and muscovado sugars, egg and butter. Process the ingredients using a hand-held blender with a kneading attachment, at first briefly on the lowest setting, then for approximately 5 minutes on the highest setting. Then knead on a work surface to form a smooth dough.

	For the filling
5 tbsp white wine **50 g (2 oz) demerara sugar** **2 tsp muscovado sugar** **¼ tsp lemon essence** **pinch ground cinnamon** **pinch ground cloves** **50 g (2 oz) raisins** **350 g (12 oz) (nett weight) peeled, cored and sliced apples**	Bring to the boil the wine, sugars, lemon essence, cinnamon, cloves and raisins. Stew the prepared apples in this mixture for about 5 minutes, then drain in a colander and allow to cool.
	Lightly dust the risen yeast dough with flour, remove from the bowl and, on the work surface, thoroughly knead into the shortcrust pastry. Roll out to a thickness of about ½ cm (¼ inch) and cut out 16 10 x 10 cm (4 x 4 inch) squares. Cut eight of the squares at 1cm (½ inch) intervals, but don't cut right to the edge so that the squares stay together. Place the filling on the whole squares, leaving a 1 cm (½ inch) edge all around.
1 egg yolk, beaten with **2 tbsp condensed milk**	Brush this edge with the beaten egg yolk and condensed milk, place the cut squares on top, pressing down the edges. Place the parcels on a baking sheet lined with non-stick baking paper. Once again leave the dough to prove in a warm place until it has risen visibly, then brush with the remaining egg/milk mixture.
Oven temperatures	
Conventional oven	170–200°C/350–400°F (preheated)
Fan-assisted oven	160–170°C/335–350°F (not preheated)
Gas oven	mark 3–4 (preheated)
Baking time	about 15 minutes.
2 tsp ground cashews	Sprinkle with the ground cashew nuts straight away and eat warm.
Serving suggestion	Serve with custard.

Puff paste is rich in fat; it is made without sugar, which makes it very versatile.

Puff paste is very time-consuming to prepare, as the dough has to be rolled out repeatedly. This repeated rolling out produces layers with thin layers of butter in between. Through the heating action of baking, the air contained in the dough expands, the water turns to steam and the butter melts. This causes the layers to rise, producing the characteristic flaky texture.

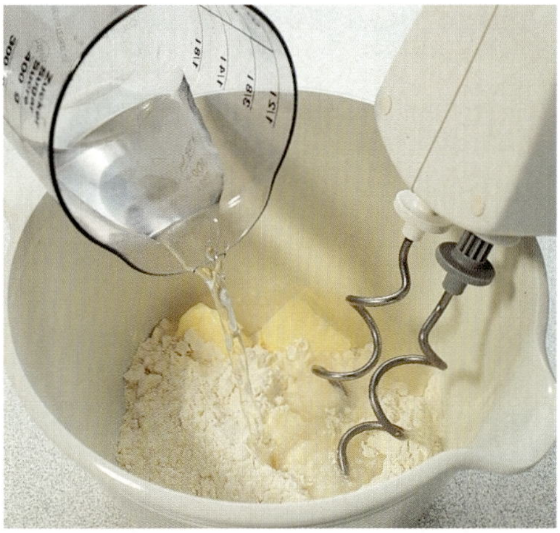

Step-by-step instructions

Assemble the ingredients and weigh and measure them. Sift the flour into a mixing bowl and add a little fat, salt, vinegar and water. **Process the ingredients using a hand-held blender with a kneading attachment**, at first briefly on the lowest setting, then thoroughly on the highest setting to make a smooth dough. Shape the dough into a ball, wrap in clingfilm and chill for 30 minutes.

Using a hand-held blender with a kneading attachment, process the butter with a little flour. Knead into a uniform mixture, first using the lowest, then the highest setting. Dust the work surface with flour and **roll out the butter mixture to form a square 12 x 12 cm (4½ x 4½ inch).**

Roll out the dough to form a 25 x 12 cm (10 x 4½ inch) rectangle and place the rolled-out butter mixture on one half of the dough.

Fold over the other half of the dough and press down the edges.

Roll out the dough to form a rectangle 1 cm (½ inch) thick. **Fold over in thirds lengthways and turn the rectangle 90° (one-quarter turn).**

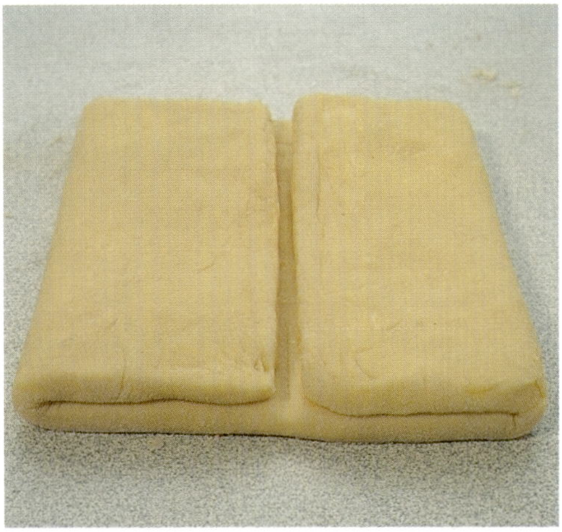

Once again roll out the dough to form a rectangle 1 cm (½ inch) thick, **fold over in quarters lengthways, cover and chill for 30 minutes.**

Roll out the dough into a rectangle 1 cm (½ inch) thick, fold over in thirds lengthwise and turn 90° (one-quarter turn).

Once again roll out the dough to form a rectangle 1 cm (½ inch) thick, fold over in quarters lengthways, cover and chill for 30 minutes.

Baking puff paste

Before baking, grease the baking sheet and always moisten it with cold water. After baking, immediately remove the pastry from the tray and leave to cool on a cake rack.

Basic recipe
Grundrezept

225 g (8 oz) plain flour **25 g (1 oz) butter** **1/4 tsp salt** **1/2 tbsp vinegar** **125 ml (4 fl oz) lukewarm water**	Sift the flour into a mixing bowl and add the butter, salt, vinegar and water. Process the ingredients using a hand-held blender with a kneading attachment, at first briefly on the lowest setting, then thoroughly on the highest setting. Cover the dough with clingfilm and leave to prove for 30 minutes.
225 g (8 oz) ice-cold butter **25 g (1 oz) plain flour**	Place the butter in a mixing bowl and add the flour. Using a hand-held blender with a kneading attachment, process both ingredients on the highest setting to produce a uniform mixture. Roll out on the work surface, dusted with flour, to form a 12 x 12 cm (4½ x 4½ inch) square.

a. Roll out the dough to form a 25 x 12 cm (10 x 4½ inch) rectangle and place the rolled-out butter mixture on one half of the dough. Fold over the other half of the dough and press down the edges.

b. Roll out the dough to form a rectangle 1 cm (½ inch) thick. Fold over in thirds lengthways and turn 90° (one-quarter turn).

c. Once again roll out the dough to form a rectangle 1 cm (½ inch) thick, fold over in quarters lengthways, cover and chill for 30 minutes.

Repeat steps b and c once more.

Continue and bake as per recipe.

Variation Use strong plain flour instead of plain flour.

Shoe Soles

traditional

Schuhsohlen, gefüllt (Photo)

	For the dough
300 g (10½ oz, 5 sheets) puff paste	Defrost the puff paste, covered, at room temperature; lay the sheets on top of one another.
or	
½ basic puff paste recipe **sugar**	Using half the basic recipe for puff pastry, roll out thinly and cut into circles about 6 cm (2½ inch) in diameter. Roll out each circle on sugar to form ovals. Place these on a greased baking sheet rinsed with water.
Oven temperatures	
Conventional oven	200–220°C/350–400°F (preheated)
Fan-assisted oven	170–180°C/325–350°F (not preheated)
Gas oven	mark 4–5 (preheated)
Baking time	about 10 minutes. Remove the shoe soles from the baking sheet and leave to cool.
	For the filling
250 ml (9 fl oz) double cream **2 tsp vanilla sugar** **2 tsp cream of tartar** **kirsch**	Whip the cream for ½ minute. Mix the vanilla sugar and cream of tartar and sprinkle this over the cream. Whip the cream until firm and add kirsch to taste. Pipe the cream on the underside of half of the shoe soles and place the other half on top.

Raspberry Slices

easy

Himbeerschnitten

	For the dough
300 g (10½ oz, 5 sheets) puff paste	Defrost the puff paste at room temperature, leaving it covered with a cloth; slice each sheet in half crossways and place on a greased, dampened baking sheet.
Oven temperatures	
Conventional oven	200–220°C/400–425°F (preheated)
Fan-assisted oven	170–180°C/325–350°F (not preheated)
Gas oven	mark 4–5 (preheated)
Baking time	about 15 minutes. Remove the sheets from the baking sheet and leave to cool. Using a serrated knife, carefully slice through each sheet horizontally.
	For the filling
300 g (10½ oz) raspberry jam **250 ml (9 fl oz) double cream** **2 tsp cream of tartar** **2 tsp vanilla sugar** **1 tbsp raspberry liqueur**	Spread the jam on the bottom half of the sheet. Whip the cream for 30 seconds. Mix the vanilla sugar and cream of tartar, and sprinkle on the cream. Whip the cream until firm and add the raspberry liqueur. Spread cream over the jam.

(continued on page 228)

For the icing

100 g (3½ oz) icing sugar **2 tbsp lemon juice** **2 tbsp water** **50 g (2 oz) chocolate cake covering**	Sift the icing sugar and mix with the lemon juice and water. Brush over the top halves of the puff pastry slices. Melt the chocolate cake covering in a small saucepan in a bain-marie over a low heat. Pipe stripes of the chocolate on the hardening white icing and immediately work with a toothpick to make spider's web patterns.

Pig's ears

traditional

Schweineöhrchen

300 g (10½ oz, 5 sheets) puff paste	Defrost the puff pastry, covered, at room temperature. Place the sheets on top of one another.
or	
½ basic puff paste recipe **25 g (1 oz) melted cooled butter** **50 g (2 oz) sugar** **2 tsp vanilla sugar**	Roll out ½ basic recipe for puff pastry to form a 55 x 22 cm (22 x 8½ inch) rectangle. Brush with melted, cooled butter. Combine the sugar and vanilla sugar and sprinkle over the dough. Fold the left part of the long side of the sheet into two-thirds and the right part in one-third, so that the edges touch. Then fold the sheet from the longer side in half, leaving the sheet in front of you that way. Roll out into a 30 cm (12 x 12 inch) square; fold over the left and right side into the middle, leaving a 2 cm (1 inch) gap in the middle. Place the left-hand wide edge on the right-hand edge, then chill the dough until it is hard enough to cut. Cut slices about. 1 cm (½ inch) thick and place on a greased, moistened baking sheet.
Oven temperatures	
Conventional oven	200–220°C/400–425°F (preheated)
Fan-assisted oven	170–180°C/325–350°F (not preheated)
Gas oven	mark 3–4 (preheated)
Baking time	about 10 minutes.
sugar	Remove the pastries from the baking sheet and, while hot, sprinkle with sugar.
Tip	If stored in layers, sprinkled with icing sugar in containers with closely fitting lids, the pig's ears will keep for 2-3 weeks.

Strawberry Slices

popular

Erdbeerschnitten (see photo on pages 220/221)

	For the dough
300 g (10½ oz, 5 sheets) puff paste	Defrost the puff pastry, covered, at room temperature. Place the
or	sheets on top of one another.
½ basic puff paste recipe	Use half the basic recipe for puff pastry.
	For the filling
1 packet vanilla pudding powder	Follow the packet instructions for making the vanilla pudding but
40 g (1½ oz) sugar	use the quantities of sugar, milk and cream given here. Leave to
125 ml (4 fl oz) milk	cool, stirring occasionally.
250 ml (9 fl oz) double cream	
	For the topping
750 g (1 lb 10 oz) strawberries	Wash and drain the strawberries. Hull them, halve them and
50 g (2 oz) sugar	sprinkle with sugar and leave to draw juice. Place the puff paste sheets on top of one another; first roll out to form a 34 x 30 cm (13½ x 5½ inch), then cut this into two 30 x 14 cm (12 x 5½ inch) rectangles and place these on a greased, moistened baking sheet. Cut the remaining dough into thin strips and intertwine them. Brush the edges of the sheets with condensed milk and place the
condensed milk	strips on the edges. Prick the sheets several times with a fork. Prick again during baking.
Oven temperatures	
Conventional oven	200–220°C/400–425°F (preheated)
Fan-assisted oven	170–180°C/325–350°F (not preheated)
Gas	mark 4–5 (preheated)
Baking time	15–20 minutes. Immediately after baking, remove the pastry from the baking sheet and leave to cool on a wire rack. Spread with the pudding and place the strawberries, thoroughly drained, on top.
	For the glaze
1 packet red jelly glaze	Prepare the glaze with the sugar, strawberry juice topped up with
30 g (1 oz) sugar	the water according to the packet instructions. Spread over the
250 ml (9 fl oz) strawberry juice	strawberries. Sprinkle the almonds on the long edges of the
(water added if necessary)	pastries.
1 tbsp blanched chopped almonds	

Almond Bows

Mandelschleifen

sophisticated

For the pastry

300 g (10½ oz, 5 sheets) puff paste	Defrost the puff pastry, covered, at room temperature; lay the sheets on top of one another.
or	
½ basic puff paste recipe	Use half the basic recipe for puff pastry and roll out to form a 50 x 35 cm (20 x 14 inch) rectangle

For the filling

200 g (7 oz) marzipan **1 tbsp apricot jam** **50 g (2 oz) softened margarine or butter**	Using a hand-held blender with a stirring attachment, blend the marzipan, jam and the soft margarine or butter to form to smooth mixture. Spread on one half of the dough (photo 1). Fold over the other half of the dough to make a 25 x 35 cm (10 x 14 inch) rectangle . Cut this into strips, about 15 mm (¾ inch) wide and 25 cm (10 inch) long (photo 2).
condensed milk **about 4 tsp blanched, slivered almonds**	Loosely knot the strips, place on a greased, dampened baking sheet (photo 3), brush with condensed milk and sprinkle with the almonds.

Oven temperatures	
Conventional oven	200–220°C/400-425°F (preheated)
Fan-assisted oven	180–200°C/350°F (not preheated)
Gas oven	mark 4–5 (preheated)
Baking time	about 15 minutes.
30 g (1 oz) icing sugar	Allow to cool and, before serving, dust with icing sugar.

Cream Horns

Schillerlocken (16 horns)

traditional

1 basic puff paste recipe	Prepare one quantity of the basic recipe for puff pastry (page 225). Roll out half of the dough on a floured work surface into a 30 cm x 20 cm (12 x 8 inch) rectangle . Using a cutter, slice the dough into 8 strips 2 cm (1 inch) wide. Rinse 8 cream horn moulds with cold water. Starting at the tip, wrap each strip of dough around the metal mould (photo 1) in such a way that two-thirds of the strip cover one turn around the mould and the last third overlaps the preceding turn. Use the rest of the dough in the same way to make another eight horns.
1 egg yolk **3 tbsp milk** **4 tbsp blanched, slivered almonds** **4 tbsp coarse sugar crystals**	Beat the egg yolk and milk and brush it over the horns. Mix the almonds and sugar and roll the horns in this mixture (photo 2). Place on a greased, dampened baking sheet.
Oven temperatures	
Conventional oven	200–220°C/400–425°F (preheated)
Fan-assisted oven	170–180°C/350°F (not preheated)
Gas oven	mark 4–5 (preheated)
Baking time	about 15 minutes. Allow to cool slightly, remove from the moulds and leave to cool on a wire rack.
	For the filling
500 ml (18 fl oz) double cream **2 tsp sugar** **15 g (2 tbsp) cream of tartar** **1 tbsp orange marmalade** **1 tbsp raspberry jam** **1 tbsp grated chocolate**	Whip the cream for 1 minute. Combine the sugar and cream of tartar and sprinkle this over the cream. Whip the cream until firm. Divide the cream into three portions. Mix one with the marmalade, one with the jam and one with the grated chocolate. Pipe the fillings into the horns (photo 3).

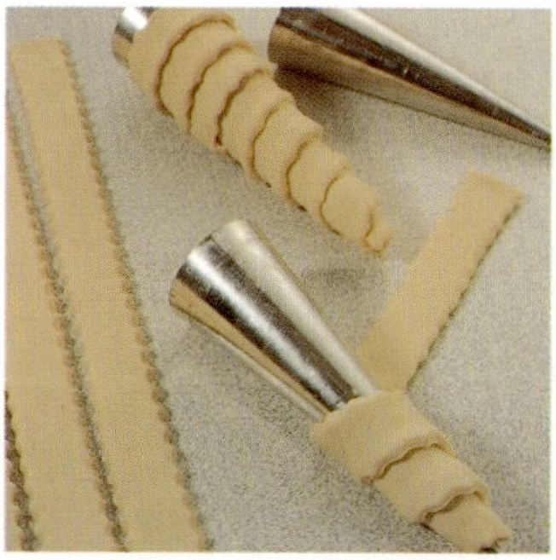

Step-by-step instructions

Using a hand-held blender with a whisking attachment, beat the egg whites on the highest setting until stiff. A cut made in the whisked egg whites with a knife should remain visible.

Slowly pour in the sugar and carefully add the remaining ingredients depending on the recipe.

Fill a piping bag with the meringue mixture and pipe into the desired shapes on a baking sheet lined with non-stick baking paper.

or

Using 2 teaspoons, place small heaps of the meringue mixture on the baking sheet.

Basic meringue recipe

Grundrezept Baiser

4 egg whites	Using a hand-held blender with a whisking attachment, whisk the egg whites on the highest setting until stiff. A cut made in the whisked egg whites with a knife has to stay visible. Add the sugar
200 g (7 oz) caster sugar	one tablespoon at a time. Fill a piping bag with the meringue mixture and pipe into the desired shapes on a baking sheet lined with non-stick baking paper. Alternatively, using 2 teaspoons, place small heaps of the meringue mixture on the baking sheet.
Oven temperatures	
Conventional oven	110–130°C/225°F (preheated)
Fan-assisted oven	about 100°C/200°F (not preheated)
Gas oven	25 minutes gas mark 1, off for 25 minutes, 25 minutes gas mark 1 (not preheated)
Baking time	70–100 minutes. The meringue should be firm but should not be allowed to take on a yellow colour.

Almond Macaroons

easy

Mandelmakronen

2 egg whites **100 g (3½ oz) caster sugar** **1 pinch ground cinnamon** **2 drops almond essence** **100 g (3½ oz) blanched, ground almonds** **75 g (3 oz) blanched, chopped almonds**	Using a hand-held blender with a whisking attachment, whisk the egg whites on the highest setting until stiff. A cut made in the whisked egg whites with a knife has to stay visible. Work in the sugar, cinnamon and almond flavouring. Carefully mix in the ground and chopped almonds on the lowest setting. Using 2 teaspoons, place small heaps of the meringue mixture on a baking sheet lined with non-stick baking paper.
Oven temperatures	
Conventional oven	130–150°C/250°F (preheated)
Fan-assisted oven	110–120°C/225°F (not preheated)
Gas oven	mark 1–2 (not preheated)
Baking time	30–35 minutes.

Meringue fruit tartlets

traditional

Baiser-Obst-Törtchen (see photo on pages 234/235)

For the filling

500 g (18 oz) canned gooseberries
500 g (18 oz) strawberries
3 tsp sugar

Drain the gooseberries, reserving the juice. Wash, drain, hull and halve the strawberries and sprinkle with the sugar.

For the meringue

2 egg whites
100 g (3½ oz) caster sugar

Using a hand-held blender with a whisking attachment, whisk the egg whites on the highest setting until stiff. A cut made in the whisked egg whites with a knife has to stay visible. Gradually add the sugar. Fill the meringue mixture into a piping bag with a serrated nozzle. Using a spiral motion, pipe tarts with a diameter of about 7 cm (2¾ inch), about 2 cm (1 inch) high around the edges, on a baking sheet lined with non-stick baking paper. For each tartlet, pipe one dot as a hat.

Oven temperatures
Conventional oven 110–130°C/225°F (preheated)
Fan-assisted oven about 100°C/200°F (not preheated)
Gas oven 25 minutes gas mark 1, off for 25 minutes, 25 minutes gas mark 1
Baking time about 70 minutes.
Allow to cool.

For the glaze

1 packet clear jelly glaze (without added sugar)
250 ml (9fl oz) juice from canned gooseberries (water added if necessary)

Following the packet instructions, use the glaze powder (without extra sugar) and gooseberry juice (topped up with water if necessary) to make up the glaze. Spread on the fruit.

whipped cream

Serve with whipped cream.

Tip You can vary the fruit as desired: try fresh gooseberries, morello cherries, stewed rhubarb or mixed berries. Use red glaze if using red fruit.
Can also be served with vanilla ice cream.

Chocolate kisses

for guests

Busserl

2 egg whites 100 g (3½ oz) caster sugar 1 tbsp cocoa powder 50 g (2 oz) finely chopped semi-sweet chocolate	Using a hand-held blender with a whisking attachment, whisk the egg whites on the highest setting until stiff. A cut made in the whisked egg whites with a knife has to stay visible. Gradually add the sugar. Sift the cocoa powder onto the egg whites. Add the chopped chocolate and fold in carefully, using the lowest setting. Using 2 teaspoons, place walnut-sized heaps of the meringue mixture on a baking sheet lined with non-stick baking paper.
Oven temperatures	
Conventional oven	110–130°C/225°F (preheated)
Fan-assisted oven	about 100°C/200°F (not preheated)
Gas oven	mark 1–2 (not preheated)
Baking time	25–35 minutes.

Chocolate coconut kisses

easy

Raspeli

3 egg whites 200 g (7 oz) caster sugar 2 tbsp cocoa powder 150 g (5½ oz) desiccated coconut	Using a hand-held blender with a whisking attachment, whisk the egg whites on the highest setting until stiff. A cut made in the whisked egg whites with a knife has to stay visible. Gradually add the sugar. Sift the cocoa powder on to the egg whites. Add the desiccated coconut and fold in carefully, using the lowest setting. Using 2 teaspoons, place walnut-sized heaps of the meringue mixture on a baking sheet lined with non-stick baking paper.
Oven temperatures	
Conventional oven	130–150°C (preheated)
Fan-assisted oven	110–130°C (not preheated)
Gas oven	mark 1–2 (not preheated)
Baking time	about 25 minutes.
Tip	Meringues will keep for 3-4 weeks in metal containers with closely fitting lids.

Ice cream gateau with mocha and advocaat

for guests

Mokka-Eierlikör-Eistorte

For the shortcrust dough

150 g (5½ oz) plain flour
1 pinch baking powder
50 g (2 oz) sugar
2 tsp vanilla sugar
100 g (3½ oz) butter

Mix the flour and baking powder and sift into a mixing bowl. Add the sugar, vanilla sugar and butter. Beat with the kneading hook of a hand-held mixer, at first briefly on the lowest setting, then thoroughly on the highest. Then knead to a smooth dough on the work surface.

Roll out the dough on a 28 cm (11 inch) springform base, prick several times with a fork and place the edge of the springform mould around it.

Oven temperatures	
Conventional oven	200–220°C/400–425°F (preheated)
Fan-assisted oven	about 170°C/350°F (not preheated)
Gas oven	mark 3–4 (preheated)
Baking time	about 15 minutes.

Immediately after baking, loosen the pastry from the springform base. Leave to cool down on the base.

For the meringue

4 egg whites
200 g (7 oz) caster sugar

Line 4 baking sheets with non-stick baking paper. Draw three circles with a diameter of 28 cm (11 inch), one on each baking sheet. Using a hand-held blender with a whisking attachment, whisk the egg whites on the highest setting until stiff. Gradually add the sugar. Fill a piping bag with a round nozzle with 3 tablespoons of the mixture. Divide the remaining mixture into three portions and draw three circles with a diameter of 28 cm (11 inches). Pipe the meringue mixture inside each circle until it covers the whole area inside the circle (photo 1). Use any leftover meringue to pipe little shapes (circles, hearts, etc.) on the fourth baking sheet.

(continued on page 242)

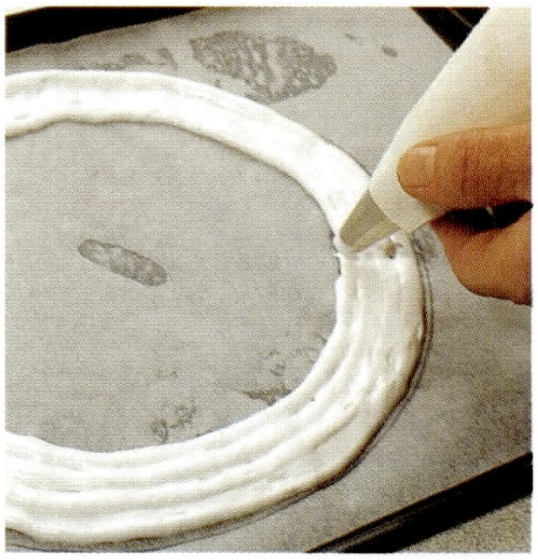

Oven temperatures	
Conventional oven	100–110°C/225°F (preheated)
Fan-assisted oven	100–110°C/200°F (preheated)
Gas oven	mark 1; turn off the oven after 30 minutes but leave meringues in the oven for about another 20 minutes
Baking time	about 75 minutes.

Store the meringues in metal tins with closely fitting lids (or wrapped in aluminium foil) until you are ready to assemble the gateau. This will prevent the meringues from going soft.

For the cream filling

1 l (1¾ pints) double cream
1 ½ tbsp cream of tartar
4 tsp vanilla sugar
4 tbsp Advocaat
2 tsp instant coffee
1 tbsp cold water

Whip the cream with the whipping cream preparation and vanilla sugar. Stir the advocaat into a quarter of the cream. Dissolve the instant coffee in the cold water and stir into one third of the remaining cream.

3 tbsp redcurrant jelly
cocoa powder

Spread the currant jelly on the shortcrust base, place one of the meringue circles on top of it; spread with the Advocaat cream and place the second meringue circle on top; spread this with the mocha cream (photo 2) and place the third circle on top (photo 3). Spread half of the remaining cream on top. Fill the remaining cream into a piping bag with a round nozzle and use it to decorate the edge of the gateau. Put the gateau in the deep freeze (ideally overnight); allow to freeze. Remove from deep freeze about 90 minutes before serving. Just before serving, decorate the gateau with the meringue shapes and dust with cocoa powder.

Tip The gateau can be prepared several days ahead and kept frozen.

Hazelnut macaroons

easy

Haselnußmakronen

4 egg whites
200 g (7 oz) caster sugar
1 pinch ground cinnamon
4 drops almond essence
200 g (7 oz) flaked hazelnuts
150 g (5½ oz) ground hazelnuts

Using a hand-held blender with a whisking attachment, whisk the egg whites on the highest setting until stiff. A cut made in the whisked egg whites with a knife has to stay visible. Gradually add the sugar, cinnamon and almond flavouring. Add the flaked and ground hazelnuts and fold in carefully, using the lowest setting.

Using 2 teaspoons, place walnut-sized heaps of the meringue mixture on a baking sheet lined with non-stick baking paper.

Oven temperatures	
Conventional oven	130–150°C/250°F (preheated)
Fan-assisted oven	110–130°C/225°F (not preheated)
Gas oven	mark 1–2 (not preheated)
Baking time	20–25 minutes.

Basle hearts

Baseler Herzen

traditional

For the dough

- 2 egg whites
- 250 g (9 oz) sugar
- 2 tsp vanilla sugar
- 2 tbsp cocoa powder
- 2 tsp ground cinnamon
- ½ tsp ground cloves
- ¼ tsp rum essence
- 15 g (½ oz) melted and cooled butter or margarine
- 250 g (9 oz) unblanched, ground almonds
- ½ tsp baking powder

Using a hand-held blender with a whisking attachment, cream the egg whites with the sugar and vanilla sugar on the highest setting. Carefully mix in the cocoa powder, cinnamon, cloves, rum essence and melted and cooled butter or margarine. Mix the unblanched ground almonds with the baking powder and stir into the egg white mixture to produce a stiff dough. Roll out the dough to a thickness of about 5 mm (¼ inch) on a work surface lightly dusted with flour. Cut out heart shapes and place on a greased baking sheet.

Oven temperatures	
Conventional oven	170–200°C/350–400°F (preheated)
Fan-assisted oven	150–180°C /350°F (not preheated)
Gas oven	mark 3–4 (preheated)
Baking time	about 10 minutes.

For the icing

- 200 g (7 oz) sifted icing sugar
- 2-3 tbsp hot water

Combine the water and sifted icing sugar to produce a thick icing. After baking, carefully loosen the hearts from the baking sheet and ice while still warm.

Wasps' nests

traditional

Wespennester (photo)

3 egg whites
250 g (9 oz) caster sugar
2 tsp vanilla sugar
125 g (4½ oz) grated chocolate
250 g (9 oz) blanched, chopped almonds

Use an electric whisk to whisk the egg whites on the highest setting until stiff. A cut made in the whisked egg whites with a knife should remain visible (photo 1). Gradually add the sugar and vanilla sugar. Carefully fold in the grated chocolate and chopped almonds, using the lowest setting (photo 2). Using 2 teaspoons, place small heaps of the mixture on a baking sheet lined with non-stick baking paper (photo 3).

Oven temperatures
Conventional oven 130–150°C/325°F (preheated)
Fan-assisted oven 110–130°C/250°F (not preheated)
Gas oven mark 1–2 (not preheated)
Baking time about 25 minutes.

Coconut macaroons

Kokosmakronen

200 g (7 oz) desiccated coconut
4 egg whites
200 g (7 oz) caster sugar
1 pinch ground cinnamon
2 drops almond essence

Lightly toast the desiccated coconut on a baking sheet and leave to cool. Whisk the egg whites until stiff. A cut made in the whisked egg whites with a knife has to stay visible. Gradually add the sugar, cinnamon and almond essence. Carefully fold the desiccated coconut into the egg whites (do not stir). Using 2 teaspoons, place small heaps of the mixture on a greased baking sheet.

Oven temperatures
Conventional oven 130–150°C/300°F (preheated)
Fan-assisted oven about 120°C/250°F (not preheated)
Gas oven mark 1–2 (not preheated)
Baking time 20–25 minutes.

AUTHENTICS

Dough types suitable for deep-frying:

The following dough types can be used for deep-frying:
- choux paste (pages 184-190)
- shortcrust dough (pages 54-59)
- quark and oil dough (pages 170-173)
- yeast dough (pages 92-97)

A large saucepan, chip pan or a deep fat fryer are suitable for deep-frying.

Fat for deep-frying:
Using the right type of fat is critical. Most suitable is a neutral, 100 per cent plant-based fat such creamed coconut. Always use oil on its own, never mix it with solid fat.
Fill the deep fat fryer with enough fat to allow the pastries to be fully immersed. Different types of deep-fried foods (such as fish and pastries) can be fried consecutively in the same fat or oil. The high temperature of the frying medium prevents the transfer of flavours.
Clean the fat or oil after deep-frying by pouring it through a metal sieve lined with kitchen paper. Fat or oil can be reused 6-10 times.

Temperature:
Fat or oil for deep-frying should be neither too hot nor too cold when the dough is placed in it. If it is too hot, the dough will brown too quickly, won't rise properly and will remain doughy inside. If the fat is too cold, the dough will absorb too much fat. The fat may start to bubble when the dough is put into it and it may bubble so violently that fragile items are literally torn apart. As soon as the fat starts bubbling, the heat needs to be increased. Do not place too many items in the fat at once. Be careful when adding fresh fat or oil, as this will cause the fat or oil to cool down.

The temperature of fat or oil should always be checked before new items are added. The temperature is right if bubbles form around the handle of a wooden spoon held in the fat. The correct temperature for deep frying is around 170–190°C (330–375°F).

After frying, drain fried items on kitchen paper.

Nut doughnuts

easy

Nußkrapfen (see photo on pages 246/247)

For the dough

375 ml (13 fl oz) water
100 g (3½ oz) margarine or butter
1 tsp sugar
1 pinch salt
250 g (9 oz) plain flour
2 tbsp cornflour
7 eggs
1 tsp baking powder
100 g (3½ oz) chopped hazelnuts
100 g (3½ oz) chopped walnuts
150 g (5½ oz) raisins

Ideally in a long-handled saucepan, boil the water, margarine or butter, sugar and salt. Mix and sift the flour and cornflour. Remove the liquid from the heat and, all in one go, tip the flour into the liquid. Stir to produce a smooth ball. Stirring, heat for about 1 minute. Immediately place the hot ball into a mixing bowl. Process using a hand-held blender with a kneading attachment on the highest setting. Gradually mix in the eggs. Work the baking powder into the cooled dough. Finally work in the chopped walnuts and hazelnuts and the raisins.

fat or oil for deep-frying
sugar mixed with cinnamon
icing sugar

Using a tablespoon, shape small pieces of the doug. Deep-fry in enough hot fat to allow them to float and cook for 6-8 minutes. Drain the nut doughnuts and roll them in a mixture of sugar and cinnamon or dust with icing sugar.

Kindling

Hobelspäne

For the shortcrust dough

500 g (1 lb 2 oz) plain flour
1 tsp baking powder
100 g (3½ oz) sugar
a few drops of lemon essence
½ tsp rum essence
3 eggs
4 tbsp milk or water
125 g (4½ oz) margarine or butter

Mix the flour with the baking powder and sift into a mixing bowl. Add the sugar, lemon essence, rum essence, eggs, milk or water and margarine or butter.

Process the ingredients using a hand-held blender with a kneading attachment, first briefly on the lowest setting, then thoroughly on the highest setting. Then knead on a work surface to produce a smooth dough. Roll out thinly. Cut into strips about 2 x 6 cm (1 x 2½ inch). Make a slit in the middle of each strip and pull one end through it.

fat or oil for deep-frying
50 g (2 oz) icing sugar

Deep-fry in the hot fat until golden brown. Remove with a slotted spoon, drain on kitchen paper and dust with icing sugar.

Bear claws

Muzenmandeln

traditional

For the shortcrust dough

500 g (1 lb 2 oz) plain flour
2 tsp baking powder
150 g (5½ oz) sugar
¼ tsp rum essence
3 eggs
1 pinch salt
150 g (5½ oz) margarine or butter

Mix the flour with the baking powder and sift into a mixing bowl. Add the sugar, rum flavouring, eggs, salt and margarine or butter. Process the ingredients using a hand-held blender with a kneading attachment: first briefly on the lowest setting, then thoroughly on the highest setting. Then knead on a work surface to produce a smooth dough. If it is sticky, chill for a while. Roll out to about 1 cm (½ inch) thick. Shape using a bearclaw mould or with teaspoons.

fat or oil for deep-frying
granulated sugar

Deep-fry in the hot fat until golden brown. Remove with a slotted spoon, drain well on kitchen paper and, still hot, roll in sugar.

"Berliner" Doughnuts

Berliner

traditional/popular

For the yeast dough

500 g (1 lb 10 oz) plain flour
1 sachet Easyblend dry yeast
2 tbsp sugar
2 tsp vanilla sugar
3 drops almond essence
1 pinch salt
2 eggs
1 egg white
125 ml (4 fl oz) lukewarm milk
100 g (3½ oz) melted, cooled margarine or butter

Sift the flour into a mixing bowl. Thoroughly mix in the yeast. Add the sugar, vanilla sugar, almond essence, salt, eggs, egg yolk, milk and melted, cooled margarine or butter.
Combine the ingredients using a hand-held blender with a kneading attachment, first briefly on the lowest setting, then for approximately 5 minutes on the highest setting to make a dough. Leave the dough to prove in a warm place until it has visibly risen. Lightly dust with flour, take out of the bowl and knead briefly on the work surface.

1 lightly-beaten egg white
300 ml (10 fl oz) jam

Roll out the dough to a thickness of about 5 mm (¼ inch) and, using a 7 cm (3 inch) circular biscuit cutter, cut out rounds. Brush the edges of half the circles with some of the beaten egg white and place a little jam in the middle. Place the other circles on top, pressing down well around the edges. Once again, leave to prove in a warm place until visibly risen.

fat or oil for deep-frying

Deep-fry in the hot fat, turning after a minute or two to cook on both sides. Remove with a slotted spoon, drain on kitchen paper

sugar

and roll in sugar.

Tip The doughnuts can be iced. To make the icing, mix icing sugar with sufficient lukewarm water to produce a spreadable icing.

Eberswald rings
Eberswalder Spritzkuchen

traditional

For the choux paste

250 ml (9 fl oz) water
50 g (2 oz) margarine or butter
150 g (5½ oz) plain flour
2 tbsp cornflour

Ideally in a long-handled saucepan, bring to the boil the water and margarine or butter. Mix and sift the flour and cornflour. Remove the liquid from the heat and, all in one go, tip the flour into the liquid. Stir to produce a smooth ball (photo 1). Stirring, heat for about 1 minute. Immediately place the hot ball into a mixing bowl.

25 g (1 oz) sugar
2 tsp vanilla sugar
4-6 eggs

1 tsp baking powder

fat or oil for deep-frying

Process using a hand-held blender with a kneading attachment on the highest setting. Gradually mix in the sugar, vanilla sugar and eggs. How many eggs you need depends on the consistency of the dough. It should be very shiny and drop off a spoon leaving long trails. Work the baking powder into the cooled dough. Cut out 10 x 10 cm (4 x 4 inch) squares of non-stick baking paper and grease them. Put the dough into a piping bag with a wide nozzle. Pipe rings on to the greased squares (photo 2). Put the rings on the paper into the deep fat or oil. Remove the paper as the ring floats off it.

Deep-fry the rings on both sides until golden brown (photo 3). Remove with a slotted spoon and drain on kitchen paper.

For the icing

200 g (7 oz) icing sugar
2 tbsp lemon juice
a few tbsp warm water

Sift the icing sugar and stir in the lemon juice and enough hot water to make a thick icing. Ice the rings.

Plum dumplings

popular

Pflaumenkrapfen

For the quark and oil dough

- 150 g (5½ oz) plain flour
- 4 tsp baking powder
- 75 g (3 oz) low-fat soft cheese
- 50 ml (2 fl oz) milk
- 50 ml (2 fl oz) vegetable oil
- 40 g (1 ½ oz) sugar
- 2 tsp vanilla sugar
- ½ tsp butterscotch flavouring
- 1 pinch salt

Mix the flour with the baking powder and sift into a mixing bowl. Add the low-fat soft cheese, milk, oil, sugar, vanilla sugar, butterscotch flavouring and salt. Process the ingredients using a hand-held blender with a kneading attachment, set on the highest setting, for about 1 minute (not too long, or the dough will become sticky). Then shape into a roll on the floured work surface.

For the filling

- 10-15 medium to large plums
- 10-15 sugar lumps
- ground cinnamon

Wash the plums, remove stalks, pat dry and remove stones. Roll the sugar cubes in cinnamon and put inside the plums.

Cut the dough into 10-15 even-sized pieces and wrap each piece round a plum. Press together well.

- fat or oil for deep-frying
- sugar

Deep-fry the dumplings, floating them the hot fat until golden brown. Remove with a slotted spoon, drain well on kitchen paper and, if desired, roll in sugar while still hot.

For the sauce

- 300 g (10½ oz) stoned plums
- about 2 tbsp sugar
- about 1 tbsp plum brandy

Purée the stoned plums in a food processor. Add sugar and plum brandy to taste.

Marzipan stollen

sophisticated

Marzipanstollen **(see photo on pages 258/259)**

For the yeast dough

375 g (13 oz) raisins **4 tbsp rum**	Drizzle the rum over the raisins and leave to soak for several hours (ideally overnight).
1 sachet Easyblend dry yeast **1 tsp sugar** **150 ml (5½ oz) lukewarm milk**	In a small bowl, thoroughly mix the yeast and sugar with the lukewarm milk. Leave at room temperature for about 15 minutes.
375 g (13 oz) strong plain flour **75 g (3 oz) sugar** **2 tsp vanilla sugar** **1 pinch salt** **2 pinch ground cardamom** **2 pinch ground star anise** **1 egg** **150 g (5½ oz) softened margarine or butter**	Sift the flour into a mixing bowl and make a well in the centre. Put the sugar, vanilla sugar, salt, cardamom, star anise, egg and very soft margarine or butter around the edge of the flour. Pour the yeast mixture into the well. Gradually incorporate the ingredients using a hand-held blender with a kneading attachment, first briefly on the lowest setting, then for approximately 5 minutes on the highest setting to make a dough. Cover the dough and leave to prove in a warm place until it has visibly risen.
100 g (3½ oz) candied lemon or citron peel, chopped **100 g (3½ oz) blanched, chopped almonds** **200 g (7 oz) marzipan**	Briefly knead the dough on a lightly-floured work surface, working in the rum-soaked raisins, candied peel and almonds. Roll out the dough into a rectangle 30 x 20 cm (12 x 8 inch). Thoroughly knead the marzipan and roll out to a rectangle 30 x 15 cm (12 x 6 inch). Place the marzipan on the dough, leaving a little dough showing along the long edges. Roll up the dough (not too loosely) from the long side into a stollen shape. Place the stollen on a baking sheet lined with two layers of non-stick baking paper. Once again leave to prove in a warm place until visibly risen.
Oven temperatures	
Conventional oven	preheat at 250°C/500°F, bake at 150–170°C/300–350°F
Fan-assisted oven	preheat at 220°C/425°F, bake at about 150°C/300°F
Gas oven	mark 2–3 (preheated)
Baking time	45–55 minutes.
100 g (3½ oz) melted butter **50g (2 oz) sifted icing sugar**	Immediately after baking, brush the stollen with half of the melted butter and dust with icing sugar. Repeat.

Fruit cake

popular

Früchtekuchen

125 g (4½ oz) hazelnuts 125 g (4½ oz) dried figs 3 eggs 125 g (4½ oz) sugar 2 tsp vanilla sugar ¼ tsp rum essence 1 pinch ground cinnamon	Halve the hazelnuts and dice the figs. Beat the eggs with a hand-held blender with a stirring attachment, on the highest setting, for 1 minute. Mix the sugar and vanilla sugar and add gradually to the beaten eggs, while processing for a further minute. Process for about 2 more minutes. Briefly mix in the rum flavouring and cinnamon.
125 g (4½ oz) plain flour 50 g (2 oz) cornflour 1 tsp baking powder 60 g (2¼ oz) blanched, chopped almonds 250 g (9 oz) raisins 125 g (4½ oz) candied citron or lemon peel	Combine the flour, cornflour and baking powder, sift them and gradually work the dry ingredients into the egg mixture, using the lowest setting of the whisk, along with the almonds, raisins and candied peel. Transfer the dough to a greased 30 x 11 cm (12 x 4¼ inch) loaf tin.
Oven temperatures	
Conventional oven	170–200°C/350–400°F (preheated)
Fan-assisted oven	about 150°C/300°F (not preheated)
Gas oven	mark 2–3 (not preheated)
Baking time	70–90 minutes.

Cinnamon stars

traditional

Zimtsterne

3 egg whites 250 g (9 oz) icing sugar	Whisk the egg whites using a hand-held blender with a stirring attachment, on the highest setting. Sift the icing sugar and stir in gradually. Reserve two heaped tablespoons of the egg white mixture for icing the stars.
2 tsp vanilla sugar 3 drops almond essence 1 tsp ground cinnamon 275-325 g (9 ½-11½ oz) unblanched, ground almonds or hazelnuts icing sugar a few drops of water	Carefully and on the lowest setting, work the vanilla sugar, almond essence, cinnamon and half the almonds or hazelnuts into the remaining egg white mixture. Knead in enough of the remaining almonds or hazelnuts to leave the dough barely sticky. Roll out the dough to a thickness of about ½ cm (¼ inch) on a work surface dusted with icing sugar. Cut out stars, place on a cookie sheet linked with non-stick baking paper and brush with the reserved egg white mixture. The icing should be liquid enough to be smoothed onto the stars. If necessary, add a few drops of water.

Oven temperatures	
Conventional oven	130–150°C/300°F (preheated)
Fan-assisted oven	about 120°C/250°F (not preheated)
Gas oven	mark 1–2 (not preheated)
Baking time	20–30 minutes. The underside of the stars should still feel a little soft after baking.

Tip Cinnamon stars are best stored in cardboard boxes.

Nuremberg spice biscuits

Nürnberger Elisenlebkuchen

(sufficient for about 40 rice paper circles, about 6 cm (2½ inches) in diameter)

	For the sponge batter
75 g (3 oz) candied orange or lemon peel **125 g (4½ oz) unblanched almonds**	Finely dice the orange or lemon peel. Grind the almonds.
2 eggs **200 g (7 oz) caster sugar** **2 tsp vanilla sugar** **1 pinch ground cloves** **¼ tsp rum essence** **1-2 drops lemon essence**	Using a hand-held blender with a stirring attachment on the highest setting, beat the eggs for 1 minute. Mix the sugar and vanilla sugar and gradually add them to the beaten eggs, while processing for a further minute; continue processing for about 2 more minutes. Stir in the cloves, rum essence and lemon essence.
1 pinch baking powder **75-125 g (3-4½ oz) ground hazelnuts***	Mix the almonds with the baking powder and, together with the orange/lemon peel and the required amount of hazelnuts*, work into the egg mixture to produce a spreadable dough. Place a heaped teaspoon of the dough on each rice paper circle and, using a knife dipped in water, spread the batter into a mound to cover the whole circle. Place on a baking sheet.
Oven temperatures	
Conventional oven	130–150°C/300°F (preheated)
Fan-assisted oven	about 120°C/250°F (not preheated)
Gas oven	mark 1–2 (preheated)
Baking time	25–30 minutes.
	For the pale icing
150 g (5½ oz) icing sugar **1-2 tbsp hot water**	Sift the icing sugar and stir in enough hot water to produce a thick glaze.
	For the dark icing
75 g (3 oz) dark chocolate **10 g (¼ oz) creamed coconut**	Using a small saucepan in a bain-marie over a low heat, melt the chocolate and creamed coconut to produce a smooth icing. Immediately after baking, brush one half of the gingerbread biscuits with the light, the remainder with the dark icing.

* The amount of hazelnuts required depends on the size of the eggs.

Rolled oat biscuits

Haferflockenplätzchen

75 g (3 oz) margarine or butter **125 g (4½ oz) rolled oats** **75 g (3 oz) sugar** **1 egg** **3-5 drops almond essence**	Melt the margarine or butter and lightly brown the oats, stirring constantly. Add 1 tablespoon of the sugar and briefly brown with the oats. Leave the oats to cool. Using a hand-held blender with a stirring attachment, beat the egg for 1 minute. Gradually add the remaining sugar and the almond essence and continue processing for about 2 more minutes.
50 g (2 oz) plain flour **1 tsp baking powder**	Mix the flour and baking powder and sift over the egg mixture. Add the cooled oats and briefly blend in using the slowest speed. Using 2 teaspoons, place walnut-sized pieces of the dough onto a greased cookie sheet.
Oven temperatures	
Conventional oven	180–200°C/375–400°F (preheated)
Fan-assisted oven	160–180°C /350°F (not preheated)
Gas oven	mark 3–4 (preheated)
Baking time	12–15 minutes.

Christmas tree pretzels

Christbaumbrezeln

100 g (3½ oz) margarine or butter **200 g (7 oz) sugar** **2 tsp vanilla sugar** **1 pinch of salt** **1 egg** **1 egg white** **500 g (1 lb 2 oz) plain flour** **15 g (1 tbsp) baking powder** **1 egg yolk** **1 tbsp milk**	Using a hand-held blender with a stirring attachment on the highest setting, cream the margarine or butter and gradually work in the sugar, vanilla sugar, salt, egg and egg white. Combine the flour and baking powder and sift them. Work in two-thirds of the flour on a medium setting and knead in the remaining flour on the work surface. Chill the dough for a while if it is sticky. Shape small batches of the dough into pencil-sized sausage shapes. Cut these into lengths of about 20 cm (8 inch) and shape into pretzels. Place on a greased baking sheet. Beat the egg yolk with the milk and brush the mixture over the biscuits.
Oven temperatures	
Conventional oven	180–200°C/375–400°F (preheated)
Fan-assisted oven	160–180°C /350°F (not preheated)
Gas oven	mark 3–4 (preheated)
Baking time	about 15 minutes.

Quark stollen

traditional

Quarkstollen

For the shortcrust dough

375 g (13 oz) raisins
100 ml (3½ fl oz) rum

Drizzle the raisins with the rum and leave to soak for several hours (ideally overnight).

500 g (1 lb 2 oz) plain flour
15 g (1 tbsp) baking powder
150 g (5½ oz) sugar
2 tsp vanilla sugar
1 pinch of salt
4 drops almond essence
1 pinch each cloves, cardamom, ginger, nutmeg, cinnamon, mixed together
2 tbsp chopped candied orange
2 eggs
150 g (5½ oz) margarine or butter
50 g (2 oz) suet, finely chopped
250 g (9 oz) quark
250 g (9 oz) blanched, ground almonds
150 g (5½ oz) candied lemon or citron peel
100 g (3½ oz) candied orange peel

Mix the flour with the baking powder and sift into a mixing bowl. Add the sugar, vanilla sugar, salt, almond essence, the ground cloves, cardamom, ginger, nutmeg and cinnamon, chopped candied orange, eggs, margarine or butter, suet and quark.

Process the ingredients using a hand-held blender with a kneading attachment. Blend briefly on the lowest setting at first, then thoroughly on the highest setting.

On a work surface, knead in the ground almonds, lemon and orange peel and the rum-soaked raisins to produce a smooth dough.

(continued on page 268)

To shape the dough into a stollen, roll up the dough and, using a rolling pin, make a lengthways depression (photo 1). Fold the left side towards the right side (photo 2) and shape the middle section with your hands (photo 3). Place the stollen on a baking sheet lined with two layers of non-stick baking paper.

Oven temperatures	
Conventional oven	Preheat at 250°C/450°F, bake at 160–180°C/325–350°F
Fan-assisted oven	Preheat at about 200°C/400°F, bake at about 150°C/300°F
Gas oven	mark 2–3 (preheated)
Baking time	50–60 minutes.

100 g (3½ oz) melted butter
50 g (2 oz) icing sugar

Immediately after baking, brush the stollen with half of the melted butter and dust with icing sugar. Repeat.

Egg biscuits

popular

Spritzgebäck (mit Eigelb)

250 g (9 oz) margarine or butter
250 g (9 oz) sugar
2 tsp vanilla sugar
3 egg yolks
1 pinch of salt
crystallised lemon or orange slices
500 g (1 lb 2 oz) plain flour
2 tsp baking powder
1 tbsp milk

Using a hand-held beater with a stirring attachment on the highest setting, cream the margarine or butter and gradually work in the sugar, vanilla sugar, egg yolks, salt and lemon or orange slices. Process until the ingredients form a uniform mixture. Mix the flour and baking powder and sieve.
Gradually work in two-thirds of the flour and the milk on a medium setting and knead in the remaining flour on the work surface. Push the dough through a forcing bag with a notched nozzle, cut to desired length and arrange the straight or ring-shaped biscuits on a baking sheet.

Oven temperatures	
Conventional oven	170–200°C/375–400°F (preheated)
Fan-assisted oven	160–180°C/325–350°F (not preheated)
Gas oven	mark 3–4 (preheated)
Baking time	about 15 minutes.

Tip Dip the ends of the biscuits in chocolate and sprinkle them with chopped pistachio nuts.

Ginger nuts

traditional

Pfefferkuchenplätzchen

250 g (9 oz) plain flour
2 tsp baking powder
175 g (6 oz) sugar
2 tsp vanilla sugar
1 pinch ground cinnamon
1 pinch ground cloves
1 pinch grated nutmeg
6 drops lemon essence
100 g (3½ oz) honey
1 egg yolk
2 tbsp milk
125 g (4½ oz) margarine or butter
1 packet chocolate pudding powder
1 tbsp chopped almonds
125 g (4½ oz) ground hazelnuts
1 egg white, beaten
chocolate chips
coarse sugar
chopped hazelnuts or walnuts
chopped almonds
finely diced candied lemon or orange peel

Mix the flour with the baking powder and sift into a mixing bowl. Add the sugar, vanilla sugar, cinnamon, cloves, nutmeg, lemon essence, honey, egg yolk, milk, margarine or butter, chocolate pudding powder, almonds and hazelnuts.
Process using a hand-held blender with a kneading attachment: first briefly on the lowest setting, then on the highest setting. Then knead into a smooth dough on the work surface.
Chill the dough for a while if it is sticky. Roll out thinly and cut out biscuits using shape cutters.

Place on a greased baking sheet. Brush with beaten egg white and, as desired, sprinkle with the chocolate chips, coarse sugar, chopped hazelnuts or walnuts, chopped almonds or finely diced orange or lemon peel.

Oven temperatures

Conventional oven	180–200°C/350–400°F (preheated)
Fan-assisted oven	160–180°C/325–350°F (not preheated)
Gas oven	mark 3–4 (preheated)
Baking time	8–10 minutes.

Variation Instead of the above decorating suggestions, decorate some of the biscuits with coloured icing sugar after baking.

Vanilla crescents

Vanillekipferl

traditional

For the shortcrust dough

- 250 g (9 oz) plain flour
- 1 pinch baking powder
- 125 g (4½ oz) sugar
- 2 tsp vanilla sugar
- 3 egg yolks
- 200 g (7 oz) margarine or butter
- 125 g (4½ oz) blanched, ground almonds

Mix the flour with the baking powder and sieve into a mixing bowl. Add the sugar, vanilla sugar, egg yolks, margarine or butter and almonds (photo 1).
Process the ingredients using a hand-held blender with a kneading attachment, first briefly on the lowest setting, then on the highest setting. Then knead into a smooth dough on the work surface. Chill the dough for a while if it is sticky.
Shape the dough into pencil-sized sausage shapes. Cut these into 5-6 cm (2-2½ inch) lengths, tapering the ends slightly and shape into crescents. Place the crescent shapes on a baking sheet (photo 2).

Oven temperatures

Conventional oven	170–200°C/350–400°F (preheated)
Fan-assisted oven	160–170°C/325–350°F (not preheated)
Gas oven	mark 3–4 (preheated)
Baking time	about 10 minutes.

- about 50 g (2 oz) icing sugar
- 2 tsp vanilla sugar

Sift the icing sugar, mix with the vanilla sugar and sprinkle over the hot biscuits (photo 3).

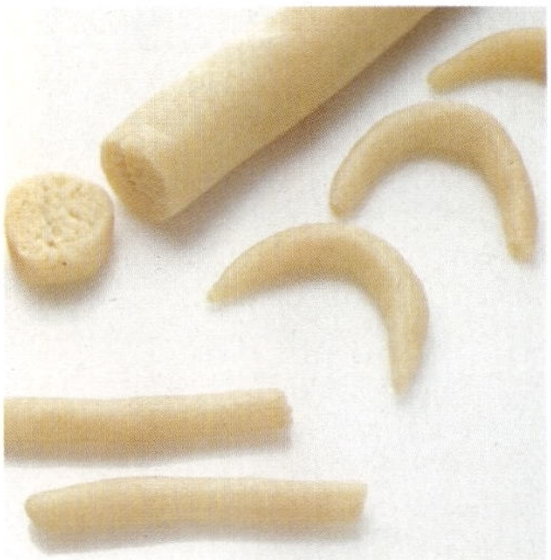

Liegnitzer

Liegnitzer (24 biscuits)

If you don't have baking rings, you can easily make your own for these biscuits: fold aluminium foil to make 12 layers of foil, each 15 cm (6 inch) long. On the top layer, draw 2 circles, side by side, about 15 cm (6 inch) in diameter. Cut them out to make 24 foil circles.
Place each circle, shiny side down, on the bottom of an upturned mug or beaker, such as a yoghurt pot. Firmly press down on the foil to make moulds with an even edge. Place the moulds on a baking sheet.

For the dough

- **200 g (7 oz) honey or syrup**
- **125 g (4½ oz) sugar**
- **1 pinch of salt**
- **65 g (2½ oz) margarine or butter**
- **2 tbsp milk**
- **2 eggs**
- **¼ tsp lemon essence**
- **ground cardamom**
- **½ tsp ground cloves**
- **1 tsp ground cinnamon**

Gently heat and melt the honey or syrup, sugar, salt, margarine or butter and milk. Pour into a mixing bowl and chill.
When almost cold, use a hand-held blender with a stirring attachment on the highest setting to beat in the eggs, lemon essence, cardamom, cloves and cinnamon.

(continued on page 274)

250 g (9 oz) plain flour **25 g (1 oz) cocoa powder** **3 tsp baking powder** **65 g (2½ oz) currants** **65 g (2½ oz) blanched, chopped almonds** **65 g (2½ oz) candied lemon peel, chopped**	Mix the flour and cocoa powder with the baking powder. Sift them together and beat in gradually, using a medium setting. On a medium setting, work in the currants, chopped almonds and chopped candied peel. Divide the dough between the foil cups (photo 1).
Oven temperatures	
Conventional oven	180–200°C/350–400°F (preheated)
Fan-assisted oven	160–180°C/325–350°F (not preheated)
Gas oven	mark 3–4 (preheated)
Baking time	10–15 minutes. Remove the biscuits from the foil immediately after baking (photo 2) and allow to cool.
175 g (6 oz) apricot jam **2 tbsp water**	Rub the jam through a sieve and bring to the boil with the water. Thinly brush onto the cooled biscuits.
	For the icing
about 200 g (7 oz) chocolate cake covering	Cut the chocolate cake covering into small pieces and stir until smooth on a low heat in a small saucepan in a bain-marie. Ice the biscuits (photo 3).
Tip	Use currant jelly or morello cherry jam instead of the apricot jam.

Nut biscuits

Nußprinten

traditional

For the topping

about 200 g (7 oz) skinned hazelnuts

Halve the skinned hazelnuts.

For the dough

125 g (4½ oz) golden syrup
50 g (2 oz) sugar
1 pinch of salt
50 g (2 oz) margarine or butter
2 tbsp milk or water
50 g (2 oz) dark brown sugar
3 drops of lemon essence
½ tsp ground star anise
½ tsp ground cloves
½ tsp ground cinnamon

Gently heat and melt the golden syrup, sugar, salt, margarine or butter and the milk or water. Pour into a mixing bowl and chill. When almost cold, use a hand-held blender with a stirring attachment on the highest setting to work in the sugar, lemon essence, star anise, cloves and cinnamon.

250 g (9 oz) plain flour
3 tsp baking powder

Mix the flour with the baking powder and sieve. Gradually work in two-thirds of the flour on a medium setting and knead in the remaining flour on the work surface to produce a smooth dough. Chill the dough for a while if it is sticky.
Roll out to a thickness of about 5 mm (¼ inch) and cut into rectangles about 2½ cm x 7 cm (1 x 2¾ inch). Place on a greased baking sheet and cover with the halved hazelnuts arranged close together.

Oven temperatures
Conventional oven: 170–200°C/350–400°F (preheated)
Fan-assisted oven: 150–180°C/300–350°F (not preheated)
Gas oven: mark 3–4 (preheated)
Baking time: about 10 minutes.

For the icing

200-250 g (8½-9 oz) chocolate cake covering
25 g (1 oz) creamed coconut

Cut the chocolate cake covering into small pieces and, on a low heat, melt with the creamed coconut in a small saucepan in a bain-marie until smooth. Ice the biscuits when cool.

Spice biscuits

Spekulatius

traditional

250 g (9 oz) plain flour 2 tsp baking powder 250 g (9 oz) sugar 2 tsp vanilla sugar 1 drop almond essence 1 pinch ground cardamom 1 pinch ground cloves ½ tsp ground cinnamon 1 pinch of salt 1 egg 100 g (3½ oz) margarine or butter 50 g (2 oz) blanched, ground almonds	Mix the flour with the baking powder and sieve into a mixing bowl. Add the sugar, vanilla sugar, almond essence, cardamom, cloves, cinnamon, salt, egg, margarine or butter and almonds. Process the ingredients using a hand-held blender with a kneading attachment, at first briefly on the lowest setting, then on the highest setting. Then knead into a smooth dough on the work surface. Chill the dough for a while if it is sticky. Roll out the dough thinly, cut out different shapes (especially animals) with biscuit cutters and place on a baking sheet. If using special biscuit moulds, press the dough into the well-floured moulds (photo 1), trim off the surplus dough or cut across the mould with a wire (photo 2). Tap the biscuits sharply so that they fall out of the moulds (photo 3).
Oven temperatures	
Conventional oven	180–200°C/350–400°F (preheated)
Fan-assisted oven	160–180°C/325–350°F (not preheated)
Gas oven	mark 3–4 (preheated)
Baking time	about 10 minutes.

Tip As a variation, before baking, brush the underside of the biscuits with water and press them into blanched, flaked almonds.

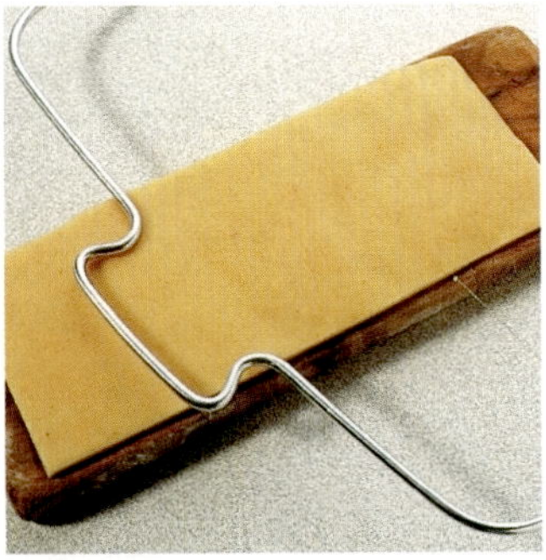

Honey cake

Honigkuchen

simple

For the dough

250 g (9 oz) honey
125 g (4½ oz) margarine or butter
2 eggs
1 tbsp mixed spice
1 tsp chopped candied citron or lemon peel

Gently heat and melt the honey and margarine or butter in a saucepan, stirring constantly. Pour into a mixing bowl and chill. When almost cold, use a hand-held blender with a stirring attachment on the highest setting to work in the eggs, gingerbread spices and lemon peel.

375 g (13 oz) plain flour
15 g (1 tbsp) baking powder
2 tsp cocoa powder
100 g (3½ oz) currants
100 g (3½ oz) ground hazelnuts

Mix the flour, baking powder and cocoa powder, sieve and add one tablespoon at a time on a medium setting. Work in the currants and ground hazelnuts and spread the dough on a well-greased baking sheet.

milk
100 g (3½ oz) blanched, slivered almonds

Brush with a little milk and sprinkle with the slivered almonds.

Oven temperatures

Conventional oven	about 170°C/325°F (preheated)
Fan-assisted oven	about 150°C/300°F (not preheated)
Gas oven	about mark 3 (preheated)
Baking time	about 20 minutes.

To glaze

5 tbsp apricot jam or passion fruit jam

Rub the apricot or passionfruit jam through a sieve and brush on the cake immediately after baking.

For the icing

200 g (7 oz) semi-sweet chocolate
25 g (1 oz) creamed coconut

Break the chocolate into small pieces and, on a low heat, melt with the creamed coconut in a small saucepan in a bain-marie until smooth.
Ice the baked cake when cooled and decorate as desired. When the icing has hardened, cut the cake into slices of the desired size and store in a container with a closely fitting lid.

There is a variety of possibilities in terms of ingredients and techniques for baking bread and rolls.

The basic ingredient is grain, whether wheat or rye, whether as wholemeal or refined flour. Sourdough and yeast are among the raising agents used to make the dough.

The shape of the bread depends on the consistency of the dough and on whether it is baked in a tin or on a baking sheet. If the bread is baked 'loose' without a tin, the dough should be firmer. The dough can then be shaped into long or round loaves.

Various grains, spices or grain flakes can be sprinkled over the bread before baking.

During baking, place a bowl of water in the oven to prevent the dough from drying out.

If you want to achieve a crusty loaf, the bread should be brushed with water just before the end of the baking time.

Sunflower seed rolls

for guests

Sonnenblumenkern-Brötchen (see photo on pages 280/281 – 12-14 rolls)

300 g (10½ oz) strong plain flour
200 g (7 oz) rye flour
1 sachet Easyblend dry yeast
1 tsp sugar
1 tsp salt
375 ml (12½ fl oz) lukewarm water
125 g (4½ oz) sourdough (leaven)
100 g (3½ oz) sunflower seeds

Combine the wheat and rye flours in a mixing bowl and thoroughly mix with the dry yeast. Add the sugar, salt, water and sourdough. Process using a hand-held blender with a kneading attachment, first on the lowest setting, then for about 5 minutes on the highest setting, to produce a smooth dough. Work in the roasted sunflower seeds at the end, reserving one tablespoon to decorate the rolls.
Leave the dough, covered, in a warm place until it has visibly risen. Lightly dust with flour, remove from the mixing bowl and briefly knead on the work surface. Roll into a thick sausage shape, cut into 12-14 pieces and shape into rolls.

Place the rolls on a greased baking sheet, brush with water and sprinkle the reserved sunflower seeds on the rolls, pressing in slightly. Once again leave to prove in a warm place until the rolls have risen visibly .

Oven temperatures

Conventional oven 200–220°C/400-425°F (preheated)
Fan-assisted oven 170–180°C/350°F (not preheated)
Gas oven about mark 4 (preheated)
Baking time about 30 minutes.

Variation Substitute shelled pumpkin seeds for the sunflower seeds.

Onion and curry bread

for guests

Zwiebel-Curry-Brot

For the yeast dough

- 500 g (1 lb 2 oz) strong plain flour
- 1 sachet Easyblend dry yeast
- 2 tsp sugar
- 1 tsp salt
- 1 1/2 tsp curry powder
- sweet paprika powder
- 250 ml (9 fl oz) lukewarm milk
- 50 g (2 oz) butter, cooled and melted
- 200-250 g (7-9 oz) onions

Put the flour in a mixing bowl and thoroughly mix with the dry yeast. Add the sugar, salt, curry powder, paprika, milk and melted, cooled butter. Process using a hand-held blender with a kneading attachment, first on the lowest setting, then for about 5 minutes on the highest setting, to produce a smooth dough.
Leave the dough, covered, in a warm place until it has visibly risen. Peel the onions and dice them finely. Lightly dust the dough with flour, remove from the mixing bowl and briefly knead on the work surface, working in the onions.

Shape into a long loaf and place on a baking sheet lined with non-stick baking paper. Make several oblique cuts, about 1 cm (½ inch) deep, in the bread.

- 1 egg yolk
- 1 tbsp milk

Beat the egg yolk with the milk and brush on the bread. Once again leave to prove in a warm place until the dough has risen visibly.

Oven temperatures

Conventional oven	about 180°C/350°F (preheated)
Fan-assisted oven	about 160°C/325°F (not preheated)
Gas oven	mark 3–4 (preheated)
Baking time	about 45 minutes.

White bread

Weißbrot

popular

	For the yeast dough
500 g (1lb 2 oz) strong plain flour 1 sachet Easyblend dry yeast 1 tsp sugar 1 tsp salt 2 eggs 1 egg yolk about 100 ml (3½ fl oz) lukewarm milk 150 ml (5½ fl oz) crème fraîche	Sift the flour into a mixing bowl and thoroughly mix with the dry yeast. Add the sugar, salt, eggs, egg yolk, milk and crème fraîche (photo 1). Process using a hand-held blender with a kneading attachment, first on the lowest setting, then for about 5 minutes on the highest setting, to produce a smooth dough (photo 2). Leave the dough, covered, in a warm place until it has visibly risen.
dry breadcrumbs	Briefly knead the dough and place in a greased loaf tin measuring 30 x 11 cm (12 x 4¼ inch) sprinkled with dry breadcrumbs. Once again leave to prove in a warm place until the dough has risen visibly. Make a cut, about 1 cm (½ inch) deep, along the length of the bread (don't use pressure, photo 3) and brush with water.
Oven temperatures	
Conventional oven	170–200°C/375–400°F (preheated)
Fan-assisted oven	about 160°C/350°F (not preheated)
Gas oven	mark 3–4 (not preheated)
Baking time	40–50 minutes.
Variation	Work 150 g (5½ oz) raisins into the dough.

Onion, bacon or herb rolls

for guests

Zwiebel-, Speck- oder Kräuterbrötchen

For the yeast dough

200 g (7 oz) strong plain flour
200 g (7 oz) plain rye flour
1 sachet Easyblend dry yeast
1 tsp sugar
2 tsp salt
1 tsp ground pepper
3 tbsp vegetable oil
300 ml (10 fl oz) lukewarm water

Combine the wheat and rye flour in a mixing bowl and thoroughly mix with the dry yeast.
Add the sugar, salt, pepper, oil and water. Process using a hand-held blender with a kneading attachment, first on the lowest setting, then for about 5 minutes on the highest setting, to produce a dough.

For onion rolls

250 g (9 oz) onions
30 g (1 oz) butter

Peel and finely dice the onion and fry in the melted butter; allow to cool slightly,

or

for bacon rolls

100 g (3½ oz) streaky bacon, finely diced
1 tbsp vegetable oil

Finely dice the streaky bacon. Heat the oil and fry the bacon; allow to cool slightly,

or

for herb rolls

1 small bunch parsley	Rinse the parsley, chives and dill, pat dry and chop finely.
1 small bunch chives	Depending on the recipe, work the ingredients into the dough
1 small bunch dill	towards the end of the kneading time.

Leave the dough, covered, in a warm place until it has visibly risen. Lightly dust with flour, remove from the mixing bowl and once again knead briefly on the work surface.

Divide into 12 even-sized pieces, shape into rolls and place onto a baking sheet lined with non-stick baking paper.

Using a pair of scissors, cut a cross about 1 cm (½ inch) deep into the top of the rolls. Once again leave to prove in a warm place until the rolls have risen visibly.

Oven temperatures	
Conventional oven	about 200°C/400°F (preheated)
Fan-assisted oven	about 180°C/350°F (not preheated)
Gas oven	mark 3–4 (preheated)
Baking time	about 25 minutes.

Tip Place a bowl with hot water in the bottom of the oven during baking.

Variation The onion rolls can also be made with roasted, dried, diced onion.

Poppyseed plaits

Mohnzöpfchen (12 plaits)

For the yeast dough

500 g (1lb 2 oz) strong plain flour	Put the flour into a mixing bowl and thoroughly mix with the dry yeast. Add the sugar, salt, oil, milk and water. Process using a hand-held blender with a kneading attachment, first on the lowest setting, then for about 5 minutes on the highest setting, to produce a smooth dough.
1 sachet Easyblend dry yeast	
1 tsp sugar	
1 tsp salt	
1 tbsp vegetable oil	
125 ml (4 fl oz) lukewarm milk	Leave the dough, covered, in a warm place until it has visibly risen. Lightly dust with flour, remove from the mixing bowl and once again knead briefly on the work surface.
250 ml (9 fl oz) lukewarm water	
	Roll into a large sausage shape and cut it into 12 pieces. Take off a third from each piece and roll each of these pieces into a sausage about 15 cm (6 inch) long. Roll the larger pieces into sausages about 30 cm (12 inch) long. Place the long sausages on the work surface in a horseshoe shape and place one of the smaller sausages inside each horseshoe.
	Plait the three strands together, press down the ends and tuck them back underneath the plait. Place on a baking sheet lined with non-stick baking paper and once again leave to prove in a warm place until the plaits have risen visibly.
poppyseeds	Brush the plaits with water and sprinkle with poppyseeds.

Oven temperatures	
Conventional oven	200–220°C/400–425°F (preheated)
Fan-assisted oven	170–180°C/350°F (not preheated)
Gas oven	about mark 4 (preheated)
Baking time	25–30 minutes.

Tip Sprinkle the plaits with sesame seeds.

Rye bread with salami
Roggenbrot mit Salami

250 g (9 oz) whole rye flour
250 g (9 oz) strong plain flour
1 sachet Easyblend dry yeast
1 tsp sugar
1 tsp salt
250 ml (9 fl oz) lukewarm water
150 g (5½ oz) finely chopped salami

For the yeast dough

Put the ground rye and flour into a mixing bowl and thoroughly mix with the dry yeast. Add the sugar, salt and water. Process using a hand-held blender with a kneading attachment: first on the lowest setting, then for about 5 minutes on the highest setting, adding in the diced salami towards the end, to produce a smooth dough.

Leave the dough, covered, in a warm place until it has visibly risen. This may take a long time, as much as five hours, as rye flour rises much more slowly than wheat flour.
Lightly dust the dough with flour, remove from the mixing bowl and knead briefly on the work surface. Shape into two longish loaves and place on a greased baking sheet. Once again leave to prove in a warm place until the loaves have risen visibly. Brush the top of the loaves with water and dust with flour.

Oven temperatures
Conventional oven about 200°C/400°F (preheated)
Fan-assisted oven about 180°C/350°F (not preheated)
Gas oven mark 3–4 (preheated)
Baking time about 40 minutes.

Tip Alternatively bake one large loaf.

Wholemeal bread
Vollkorn-Weizenbrot

425 g (15 oz) strong wholemeal flour
1 sachet Easyblend dry yeast
1 tsp caster sugar
2 tsp salt
3 tbsp vegetable oil
250 ml (9 fl oz) lukewarm water

For the yeast dough

Put the flour into a mixing bowl and thoroughly mix with the dry yeast. Add the sugar, salt, oil and water. Process using a hand-held blender with a kneading attachment: first on the lowest setting, then for about 5 minutes on the highest setting to produce a smooth dough.
Leave the dough, covered, in a warm place until it has visibly risen. Dust with flour, remove from the mixing bowl and once again knead briefly on the work surface.
Shape into a round loaf and place on a baking sheet lined with non-stick baking paper. Once again leave to prove in a warm place until risen visibly.
Make several cuts about 1 cm (½ inch) deep into the top of the loaf (don't press down) and brush with water.

Oven temperatures	
Conventional oven	about 200°C/400°F (preheated)
Fan-assisted oven	about 180°C/350°F (not preheated)
Gas oven	mark 3–4 (preheated)
Baking time	about 45 minutes. To get a crusty loaf, occasionally brush with water while baking.

Tip Knead in 2 tablespoons of mixed herbs.

Choux buns

Brandteigbrötchen

For the choux paste

250 ml (9 fl oz) water
50 g (2 oz) butter
½ tsp salt
freshly ground pepper
grated nutmeg
125 g (4½ oz) wholemeal flour
3 eggs
½ tsp baking powder
plain white flour

Ideally in a long-handled saucepan, boil the water with the butter, salt, freshly ground pepper and nutmeg. Remove from the heat and, all in one go, tip the flour into the liquid.
Stir to produce a smooth ball. Stirring, heat for about 1 minute.
Immediately place the hot ball into a mixing bowl. Process using a hand-held blender with a kneading attachment on the highest setting.
Gradually work in the eggs. Work the baking powder into the cooled dough. Using two tablespoons, place 10-12 portions of dough on a greased baking sheet dusted with white flour.

Oven temperatures	
Conventional oven	200–220°C/400–425°F (preheated)
Fan-assisted oven	170–180°C/350°F (not preheated)
Gas	mark 4–5 (preheated)
Baking time	30–40 minutes.

Serve with herb-flavoured soft cheese.

Variation

For cheese buns

100 g (3½ oz) Gouda, finely grated

Work the grated Gouda into the dough.

Cake Batters

Sweet Shortcrust

Yeast Dough

Sponge Mixture

Quark and Oil Dough

Choux Paste

Strudel Dough

Combined Doughs

Puff Paste

Meringues

Deep Fried Pastries

Christmas Baking

Bread Doughs

H

I

K

L

M

N

O

P

Q

R

S

T

V

W

Y

A

B

C

D

E

F

G

H

Environmental informance	This book and its dustjacket have been printed on paper that has been bleached without chlorine. The film coating – to protect the book from dust and dirt – consists of environmentally friendly and recyclable foil.
Information	If you have any suggestions, proposals or questions about our books, please telephone us on 49 0521 520642 or write us at: Ceres Verlag Am Bach 11 33602 Bielefeld Germany We will answer you by return.

Editors	Carola Reich, Christine Sander
English translation	Chanterelle Translations, London, England
Recipe development and text	Dr. August Oetker Research Kitchen, Bielefeld
Title photo	Brigitte Wegner, Bielefeld (Foodstyling: Eike Upmeier-Lorenz)
Inside photos	Thomas Diercks, Hamburg Brigitte Wegner, Bielefeld
Cover design	Kontur Design, Bielefeld
Concept	Björn Carstensen, Hamburg
Design	Kontur Design, Bielefeld
Reproductions	Mohndruck, Gütersloh
Typeset by	Typografika, Bielefeld
Printed by	DELO, Ljubljana, Slowenien

ISBN 3-7670-0371-6

CONVERSION TABLES

When converting quantities from metric to imperial system approximate conversions are given, i. e. 1 oz is equivalent to 28 g, and in the recipes 25 g are either rounded up to 1 oz or 30 g are rounded off to 1 oz. Please note that the metric units are more precise than the imperial ones.

Imperial	Metric
2 lb 4 oz	1 kg
1 lb 2 oz	500 g
14 oz	400 g
10½ oz	300 g
7 oz	200 g
3½ oz	100 g
2½ oz	70 g
2 oz	50 g
1½ oz	40 g
1½ oz	35 g
1 oz	25 g
½ oz	10 g

Imperial	Metric	
1½ pints	1 litre	
18 fl oz	500 ml	
14 fl oz	400 ml	
10 fl oz (½ pint)	300 ml	
7 fl oz (⅓ pint)	200 ml	
3½ fl oz	100 ml	
2 fl oz	50 ml	
	45 ml	3 tbsp
	30 ml	2 tbsp
	20 ml	1 tbsp
	10 ml	3 tsp (1 tbsp)

Fahrenheit	Celsius
475 °F	240 °C
425 °F	220 °C
400 °F	200 °C
350 °F	180 °C
325 °F	160 °C
275 °F	140 °C

A FEW COOKERY EXPRESSIONS WHICH DIFFER IN BRITISH AND U.S. TERMINOLOGY

British	US
baking sheet	cookie sheet, sheetpan
baking fat	shortening
baking tin	baking pan
biscuit	cookie
cornflour	cornstarch
double cream	heavy cream
icing sugar	powdered sugar
jelly, gelatine	gelatin
frying pan	skillet (confectioner's sugar)
plain flour	all-purpose flour
pudding powder	dessert powder
single cream	light cream
strong plain flour (for breadmaking)	all-purpose flour
tagliatelle	fettuccini
Swiss roll	jellyroll